To Jack
With kind
personal regards,
Colleen

Cathy Howe

Gordon Howe

Mark Howe

Murray Howe

Marty Howe

My Three Hockey Players

My Three Hockey Players

COLLEEN HOWE

HAWTHORN BOOKS, INC.
Publishers/NEW YORK

All text photos are from the author's personal files unless otherwise credited.

MY THREE HOCKEY PLAYERS

Library of Congress Catalog Card Number: 74-33591
ISBN: 0-8015-5294-X
1 2 3 4 5 6 7 8 9 10

To Cathy and Murray,
the rest of the team,
whose turn will come

Contents

Preface

His sparkling eyes, his toothless grin,
  His flashing blades, his will to win.
He shoots, he scores, his boyhood dream.
  His prayer: God help me help my team.
Thank you for helping him.

— "The Novice," author unknown

BEING IN SPORTS, waking up to another game day, is like being young on Christmas morning. I have had a lifetime of it. At the risk of sounding immodest, I have probably suffered, gladly, as much ice hockey as any woman alive. I have been the wife of a major leaguer, the mother of two, and the sister-in-law of one (Vic Howe, Gordie's younger brother, once a fine player with the New York Rangers).

I have seen the sparkling eyes and toothless grins, and the small boys looking up at their heroes with worship spread across their faces like peanut butter and jam.

And some challenge them. During his first season in Houston, my husband was cornered one night outside the dressing room by a ten-year-old who demanded, "Here, sign my stick."

Now, Gordie Howe is the kind of man most wives would order if there was a firm called Rent-a-Daddy. He is seldom too busy to teach a youngster manners, or to make a point about courtesy.

"What's the magic word?" he asked.

"Okay, please," and the boy held out the stick.

"Now," said Gordie, "address me by my name and put it all together."

"Gordie," the boy said, wearily, "*please* sign my goddam stick."

It wasn't exactly what he had in mind, but Gordie coughed and scribbled his autograph and walked away, confident that he had met a boy who had the will to win.

This book is meant for all of them, the novices as well as the pros, the moms and dads who raise them and the fans who root for them. This is no textbook. The technical analysis that allows sportswriters to play coach, the figures that so fascinate the incurable sports nut, are for the most part missing. I have attempted to tell, as honestly as I can, the story of a family whose life revolved around sport. What appears on these pages reflects the times and the facts only as I saw them then, or remember them now. The opinions are mine. For those, Gordie, Marty, and Mark are blameless.

Hockey has enabled us to give ourselves and our children a better life than our parents had. It has made it possible for us to see the great cities of the United States and Canada, and a good part of the world, including Russia, where I learned that there are no Bibles in hotels and Gordie's name is spelled *Xoy*.

But there really isn't much difference between a sports family and anyone else's, except that you have fewer secrets. So much of what athletes do, and what they say, happens in public. At home, you still spend much of your time trying to outwit your children. Once, years ago, when I grew tired of scolding and lecturing them about something, I said, impatiently, "Am I going to have to make a recording of this?"

Marty shook his head. "Mom," he said, "it would never sell." Most sons would probably feel the same way.

For the final form of this book I am twice indebted: To Mickey Herskowitz, one of the country's respected young writers, whose idea it was and who completed the final manuscript; and to Kathy Lewis, of *The Houston Post*, who spent long hours of interviews and research, prepared the first draft, and became my friend. The author also wishes to thank Bill Adler, for his patience and encouragement, and to Dorothy Ringler, who helped keep the office running while I was concentrating on this book — and my three hockey players.

My Three Hockey Players

1
And Daddy Makes Three

I MARRIED GORDIE HOWE for better or for worse — but not for lunch. Now, for the first time in twenty years, he wasn't gone from home half of every month. He was here, he was around, he was retired from the sport that had been his life, and he was making us both nervous.

He was forty-three and an arthritic wrist had ended his playing career. He had scored more goals and established more records than anyone in the history of the National Hockey League, and the Detroit Red Wings had rewarded him with a mindless front-office job in which his major function was to attend banquets. He always seemed to be the last one to know what was happening with the team.

He was getting what Gordie called the old mushroom treatment. "You know," he explained one night, with a small, bitter smile, "that's where they keep you in the dark and every now and then they come in and toss a little manure on you."

For a popular athlete, the adjustment to a sedentary life and the sudden semiprivacy that goes with it can be a trauma. Forget the money. They have overdosed on the strongest narcotic of all — the roar of the crowd. And it's more than that. It means letting go of your youth. Gordie was having withdrawal pains and I shared them. "Nobody teaches you," he complained, "how to retire."

It is a hurtful thing to see a proud man made to feel useless. All the more frustrating was the fact that he had come so close to fulfilling what started out as a family joke: to play pro hockey with our sons. By the time Gordie was rounding out his second decade in Detroit and going on for "one more season" and then another, his teammates began to tease him. "Hell, you'll never quit. You're hanging on for a Howe, Howe, and Howe production line."

Gordie would laugh and blink and get that *look* in his eyes. "You can't ever tell," he'd say.

But we put the dream away, we thought, on September 7, 1971, the day Gordie retired after twenty-five seasons in a Red Wings uniform. Marty, our oldest son, was then seventeen, still three years under the age minimum for the pro draft, but a year older than his father had been as a rookie in 1945. The age rules didn't exist then.

That was two cold wars and a generation gap ago. Gordie had scored his first goals when Joe Louis was heavyweight champion; Joe DiMaggio was playing center field for the Yankees; Johnny Lujack was the Notre Dame quarterback; the highest-salaried woman in the world was Betty Grable; and Ernest Hemingway had barricaded himself in Havana to write a book called *The Old Man and the Sea.*

Now it was over. At least, we consoled ourselves, Gordie had gotten to team up for one game with the boys during that final year—a charity match that raised nearly $30,000 for the March of Dimes. The Red Wings took on the Junior Wings, with Gordie on *loan* to the amateur club.

As an added touch, his oldest brother, Vern, retired from the army and living across the river in Windsor, played on the defense. Gordie was forty-three, Marty seventeen, and Mark sixteen. Even our youngest, ten-year-old Murray, made a surprise appearance and scored a goal in the last minute of play, all but bringing down the house. A crowd of 11,000 went wild over the family act, and the Howes were not exactly unaffected. "When they announced us," Gordie was to recall later, "it sounded like an Indian line: Howe, Howe, Howe. There was about a ten- to-fifteen minute standing ovation, and I looked at the boys and said, 'Wouldn't it be wonderful if it were for real.' "

At one point Gordie was tearing down the ice, and a defenseman had a good angle to take him into the boards. Mark flicked the puck behind him, just slightly, and moved toward Gordie. That little action froze the defenseman long enough to put Gordie in the clear.

Later, he rubbed his son's head and said, "Mark, that was a heck of a pass even though it was behind me."

Mark nodded and replied, "That was by *design*."

The boys had passed their father's inspection. He had been satisfied for some time that they were both pro material. The chromosomes had been passed on. It was a happy, warm, sentimental night, because we thought there would never be another like it. Gordie had already announced that this would be his last year.

The game was no longer fun. He was practically playing one-handed. Hampered by his ailing wrist, which had been slow to recover from surgery, and rib injuries, Gordie for the first time in twenty-one years wasn't among the top five scorers. The Red Wings were in turmoil, on and off the ice, and the crowds had gotten smaller and meaner. A man has to be tired and unhappy to walk away from a $100,000-a-year salary. Gordie was.

He had long been promised a front-office job with the Red Wings, and he moved into it, at half the pay, expecting to be involved in areas that would enable him to use his experience and judgment. Instead, he became a kind of vice-president in charge of paper clips. The next two years were wasted. I was unhappy because Gordie was unhappy. We began to talk about cutting the cord, getting out of hockey altogether, concentrating on the cattle and investments we had developed during the last few years.

It was on our minds that night, in the spring of 1973, when the phone rang as we were going out the door, dressed for an art auction for the benefit of the Arthritis Foundation, which I headed in Detroit that year. We stood in the doorway and looked at each other, our eyes asking if we should bother, or keep going.

Are there really people who can resist a ringing telephone? Gordie went back and picked up the receiver. I could only hear the Detroit end of the conversation, but I was catching enough to put two and two together. I decided to sit down.

The look on my husband's face was one of quizzical confusion. He hung up the phone and in a stunned voice said, "That was Doug Harvey. At this very moment the Houston Aeros are ready to walk into the World Hockey Association meetings and announce Mark as their Number One draft choice. He wanted to let us know because, once it's done, all hell is going to break loose in both leagues, and the press will be calling."

Doug Harvey was an old friend, a one-time star in the National League, now a scout and assistant coach for the Houston team in the new league that had turned pro hockey upside down.

Before we left for dinner and the art sale, which was all but forgotten, we called Mark and Marty in Toronto. Both the boys were there, playing amateur hockey for the Marlboros and living in the home of Dick and Rita Tanner, whose family had boarded young players for years. We caught Mark, who was fighting a persistent cold, at home alone. Marty and the

Tanners had gone to a banquet for the Marlies, celebrating the national junior championship the team had just won.

When we broke the news to Mark, his first words were: "What about Marty? Didn't they say anything about Marty? I'm not going unless they take him, too."

His concern for his older brother made my eyes blur. I was so proud of him. Mark had always enjoyed a little more of the limelight. He was the one the press had tagged as a carbon of his dad. As a forward, Mark had the opportunity to be a scorer. Defensemen simply don't get the glory. And Marty tended to have more than his share of hard knocks, including a bout with mononucleosis one season and a broken cheekbone that sent him to the hospital for an entire Christmas vacation.

But Mark had always been a little more intense about the game. In our trophy room we kept an oil painting of Gordie and the two older boys. They're on the ice, all in full Red Wing gear, and the boys are facing off while Gord drops the puck. The painting was copied from a photograph taken when Marty was about seven and Mark six.

One day, Gordie pointed it out to a magazine writer. "Look at it," he said, "can you see it?"

It was obvious. Marty was posing, indifferent to the piece of hard rubber that was about to land at his feet. Mark looked as if he was about to start World War III.

"The puck brings out so much in you," said Gordie, grinning. "It's the damndest thing in the world."

We had to tell Mark, "No, they didn't say anything about Marty."

Even as we talked to Mark, all hell was, indeed, breaking loose at the W.H.A. draft meetings in Chicago. It was Bill Dineen, the coach of the Aeros and once a teammate of Gordie's, who had stood and said, *"Houston drafts Mark Howe."*

7

Instantly, like a bunch of men sitting around a Monopoly table, officials of the other teams all began shouting at once, "You can't do that. You're crazy—it's illegal."

Mark was eighteen. The age at which the National Hockey League and the Canadian Amateur Association allowed their young prospects to earn wages was twenty. Everyone assumed that the W.H.A. subscribed to the same rule. But the Aeros were prepared to test it, gambling that the age limit was not only unreasonable, but probably an illegal restraint of trade.

Doug Harvey's phone call had come as a shock, but not without some previous, motherly lobbying on my part. I had, in fact, hesitated to tell Gordie about it. My temper and directness often amused him, but I think he sometimes watched me as a sea captain watches the gathering clouds, with a mixture of fear and respect.

Actually, a few weeks before the call, I had bumped into Bill Dineen outside the dressing room the night the Marlboros won the championship. Bill had spent five seasons with the Red Wings and our families had been friendly. Bill hadn't seen the boys, Mark and Marty, since they were just tots hanging around the Detroit locker room.

It seems that most of my life I have been left standing outside dressing room doors. Gordie was inside, congratulating our sons. Mark had controlled the offense and won the Most Valuable Player Award. Marty played almost perfect defense. I waited impatiently to see them, watching the door —that eternal locker room door.

This night in Montreal, Bill Dineen was there with Doug Harvey. Most of the scouts and coaches from teams in both leagues were there, in fact, because this was amateur hockey's showcase. The boys who played in this series were going to be the top draft choices. It was a livestock show.

Bill casually praised the boys' performance. I seized that opening to make what had become, that year, my favorite speech, about the unfairness of a rule that forbids the drafting of players under twenty.

"It's asinine," I said. "It's like . . . say, you had a son who played the piano. You put a lot of time and money and effort into coaching him and sending him to the best conservatories in Europe, then at age nineteen he can't play in Carnegie Hall because some rule says he's not old enough to earn a living."

My speech seemed to catch Dineen by surprise but I could tell he was taking it in.

"The hockey star," I went on, "is a genius at what he does. Some of the greats used to come into the sport at fourteen or fifteen. Gordie turned pro at sixteen. I feel strongly this should not be denied our sons." I lowered my voice. "Bill," I said, point-blank, "did your league ever reach an agreement to abide by the age minimum?"

Not to his knowledge, Bill responded after a long pause.

I smiled, said it was nice to see him, left Dineen standing there, and hurried away to meet my men.

For all I knew then my message had fallen on deaf ears — this wasn't the first time I had cornered coaches and general managers to talk about the rule. Much later, I learned that Bill and Doug had latched onto the idea and stayed up half the night discussing it.

At first, they were afraid to confide to anyone what they were thinking, for fear someone would say it couldn't be done. Finally, Bill called Jim Smith, the general manager of the Aeros and an attorney. The Aeros decided they had a legal right to draft Mark and, if they did, there was no way the league could overrule them. They went into the meeting committed to it.

What I would have given to have seen the looks on the faces of the men around that table when Houston dropped its trump card. In Detroit, sitting at dinner, our minds were out of town. Gordie and I kept wondering if another team would pick Marty. If not, why didn't Houston? What a promotion that would be—the Howe Brothers.

Meanwhile, after the early commotion had settled down, with some teams contending Houston had wasted its draft choice on Mark, the process continued. Round after round went by and the people at Houston's table studied their list of dwindling names. Then someone, Bill Dineen I think it was, slapped his forehead and said, "What the hell have we been waiting for? Marty Howe is still available. Let's grab him, too." In the twelfth round they did, and once again the room exploded.

At this point it was still strictly a test case. If in some way the moves turned out to be invalid, the Aeros would have wasted two valuable draft choices.

The night after the Houston coup, Gordie and I were scheduled to attend a banquet for the Detroit Junior Wings, a club I had brought into the Olympia Stadium with the permission of Bruce Norris, the Red Wings' owner. We felt tense and awkward walking into that banquet room. It is an understatement to say we had mixed emotions at that point. If anyone had ever had the Red Wings' insignia engraved on their hearts, the Howes had.

The National Hockey League had been a permanent presence in our lives. Gordie had been not only one of its great stars, he had been a salesman and dogged defender. His speeches always included a "don't-bite-the-hand" line and a declaration, which he meant, that everything he had he owed to hockey.

We were excited and proud of our two sons as we walked into the banquet. The "other league's" draft had been on the news all day, on radio and television. Yet people at the banquet hardly mentioned it to us. They didn't ask questions, they didn't wish the boys well, they acted as though they had never heard of it.

Pat Lannon, the comptroller of the stadium, was one of the

few to walk over to us. "I just want to congratulate you," he said, "on raising two very fine young men and I hope everything works out well for them."

But as for the rest, we were given a kind of silent treatment. Later, I turned to Gordie, hurt and confused, and said, "I just couldn't do that to someone."

It was only the first of many signs which would remind us that in sports, as in so many areas of life, people want to know what you have done for them lately.

The next day Gordie received a personal call from Clarence Campbell, the president and patriarch of the N.H.L., asking him not to let Mark and Marty sign with Houston. He said it would not only be a heavy blow to the league, but would jeopardize the entire junior hockey program.

Talk about mixed emotions. Gordie did feel allegiance to the league, to the sport, and to Mr. Campbell. He said he would have to think about it.

The next day he called back and said, "I couldn't ask that of my boy or anyone else's. I couldn't ask them to deny themselves an opportunity for which they have worked all their lives. I wouldn't want my father to ask me to give it up, and I'm not going to do it to my boys. The decision will be theirs."

In another conversation, Gordie told Mr. Campbell he would consider asking the boys to go back to the Marlboro team, if the N.H.L. would put in escrow whatever dollars the new league offered. Otherwise, it was out of the question.

So much in sports is pure hogwash. Team spirit is so often what comes in a player's envelope twice a month. But Gordie had a love of the game that was all brass bands and flags. You don't last twenty-five years, and establish the kind of career he had, without those feelings. The night he retired he told Bruce Norris, "Don't wrinkle that Number Nine jersey. I have three sons who might just want to wear it someday."

The Red Wings retired his jersey with one stipulation: The

number was there if a Howe son ever played for the Red Wings. Gordie had dreamed of that. We had thought about it and planned for it the way some parents send their sons into the priesthood.

It wasn't a cold and mercenary decision. We had to ask ourselves one question: While they waited another two years, what if they were injured? They might never be able to play again, or might handicap their careers and their future as pros. Could we ever justify that?

We called the boys and asked them to come to Detroit immediately. They were excited at the prospect of suddenly making a living at what they had been doing for nothing for many years. We sensed their excitement and it made the next steps easier to take.

We called Gerry Patterson, a business associate of ours who had advised Gordie on an endorsement contract and asked him to come to the house. We were convinced the boys needed some guidance. Not that Mark wasn't a good negotiator. When he signed with the Marlies he had asked, among other things, for $60 a week—$10 for gas money—two Marlboro blazers, "one for me and one for my brother," and a no-haircut clause that provided a $10,000 payment if his hair was hacked off.

I don't know if it was the result of his "contract" or not, but Mark didn't have the operation done on his hair that brother Marty had suffered the year before. As part of a rookie hazing ceremony, they had butchered Marty's long blond locks.

The stakes were a little higher than gas money and haircuts this time. As we talked to Gerry Patterson, a portly, jovial man, I kept thinking how different it must have been when Gordie first signed.

He had left home—a home that didn't even have indoor plumbing—without a white shirt and tie to his name. There was no one to advise him. No one to befriend him. He signed for $2,200 and the promise of a Red Wings' jacket. Here our own sons already had years of experience dealing with the press and were surrounded by people who could help them negotiate a contract in their best interests.

Gordie, Gerry, and I sat in the living room of our Bloomfield Hills home, talking about what the boys should expect in terms of dollars and guarantees. We wanted to know Gerry's hard opinion of the World Hockey Association. After all, it was only a year old then and there were questions about whether it could sustain itself.

In the middle of the conversation, Gordie rubbed his chin and said idly, "I wonder what they would offer for the three Howes?"

Gerry looked at me and I looked at him. Then we both stared at Gordie, not quite believing what our ears had just heard. Gerry recovered first. His eyes lit up and he said, "Wow! Wouldn't *that* be something! I can see the headlines now: HOWE RETURNS TO HOCKEY TO TEAM WITH SONS."

Here we were, three adults, laughing and kidding and making up this fantasy, soap-opera script about Gordie putting on his skates again. Even as we warmed to the idea and craved it, I realized it was farfetched. Gordie was forty-five, had been retired two years, and was a symbol of an age when big-league hockey consisted of six teams, all located in Canada.

But Gerry and Gordie kept talking, their voices and gestures growing more animated. All pretense of discussing the boys' contracts was put aside. They had stopped laughing.

"Look, you two," I said, finally. "Are you joking? Because if you are, let's stop talking about it."

Gordie said, "I don't know, Colleen. It would be fun."

I *knew*, from the expression on his face and the wistful sound in his voice, he *was* serious. The conversation had suddenly sobered us all. "But, Gord," I said, "in your wildest dreams, could you really think of doing this? It has been two years—and you were dog-tired then."

It was all so unreal. First, the unlikely event of our two sons being drafted by the same team. Of course, the only way Gordie would ever consider playing again would be to skate with his boys. It was a dream Gordie had abandoned. The circumstances had to be perfect. Now they were.

There were still a few ifs. At that point we didn't even know if Houston would be interested. We didn't sleep that night. We stayed awake talking and watched the first shades of gray quietly announce the morning, something we had done often in the early years of our marriage, after a big game.

We talked about the risks, as well the fun of what he was proposing to attempt. I was concerned. I felt a little tug of fear. I knew how much stamina, how many aches and pains, it would take him to prepare himself to play. He was at an age when wives worry about their husbands, when they pore over articles in *Today's Health* about stress and clip things out of the paper. In the wee hours of the morning, with dawn breaking, we both dozed off, not knowing if the step we were contemplating was the sheerest folly.

Gord and Bill Dineen had been talking back and forth long distance. Bill was keeping us up-to-date on the legality of the draft—it would be resolved in our favor but lawyers move as though slogging through knee-deep mud. During one of those calls Gordie slid it into the conversation. "Say, Bill, how would you like to have three Howes?"

At the other end there was a silence so long that Gordie thought they had been disconnected. "Bill," he said, "are you still there?"

Bill was, and once he recovered his voice the answer was, "Hell, yes!"

Dineen quickly called Jim Smith, who had no idea how old

Gord was but whose instincts told him a father-sons combination had to be great P.R. Accordingly, the Aeros placed Gordie Howe on their protected players' list.

We invited Bill Dineen and his wife Pat, Doug Harvey, and Jim Smith to our summer home at Bear Lake in upstate Michigan. The large, split-level cottage sits far back from the road on a bluff overlooking a crystal lake, which is so clear you can see forty feet below the surface. It was secluded—no radio or television, and you can stay there for a week without hearing the phone ring. In short, it was the kind of place where a harried businessman would enjoy a nice nervous breakdown.

It was where the Howes always went to fish and ski and ride Hondas and talk and think. In this pastoral setting, we began to talk about the first family plan in sports history—and more money than my brain could handle.

We picked Bear Lake as our meeting place because we wanted the friendly, informal mood we thought it would help create. I wanted to get Pat Dineen aside and ask about the city of Houston, its people, and what they thought of the hockey team. We wanted to form an impression of Jim Smith, the mod, youthful club president. Long ago we had learned that it was the people who counted in an organization. I had seen Gordie work for some unpleasant types, and I didn't want that to happen to our sons.

The Houston delegation flew into nearby Traverse City, spent the first night at a hotel there, and were waiting when we drove out the next morning to fetch them. We all had coffee in the hotel's conference room first, because Gordie and I wanted to get the hard part over with quickly. We wanted to talk dollars and find out if we were even in the same ball park. Either way, we could then drive our guests to the lake and have a relaxing weekend.

In the conference room, as we sipped our coffee, we talked about what impact a Howe threesome would have on the

Aeros, about hockey in Houston, and the new league in general. We all agreed it would be fantastic, a unique opportunity for the Howes and for the team. Then we got down to the deeper meanings of life—such as money.

Everyone left the room except for Jim Smith, Gordie, myself, and Gerry Patterson. We felt, because of the press reaction and the other pressures on us, a decision had to be reached quickly. Either this was going to work, or it wasn't. We had to know if there was any basis for continuing the discussion.

At this point we were only considering a contract for Gordie; whether he signed would not influence Marty and Mark's decision. The way we proceeded to negotiate the rough contract was hysterical. You always assume these things are done at sophisticated, highly professional levels.

But no one at that table had been through this exact scene before—a superstar father emerges from retirement and jumps leagues to play hockey with not one but two of his sons. There were no precedents.

How do you put a value on that kind of contract? Like a bunch of cigar-smoking gamblers in a poker game, no one wanted to tip his (or her) hand first. So we each wrote down a figure on a piece of paper and folded it over. Then we exchanged slips, with all the deliberate drama of, "And may I have the envelope, please?"

Jim Smith, blond and mod, a bachelor with an easy manner, opened his first. He studied it for a moment. Then a slow grin spread across his face. "Gee," he said, "I see yours is larger than mine."

We all broke into the kind of laughter that is heightened by nervousness, and at that moment we knew a deal could be made. We hadn't expected Jim to jump at the price—$1 million over four years—that we had attached to Gordie's services.

But now we had established a negotiating point. Jim could

return to Houston and tell the owners what the Howes had in mind, what it would take for us to uproot our lives. No matter how restless Gordie had been, he would still be walking away from the only job and the only home he had known in his adult lifetime.

With the uneasy chore of talking hard cash behind us, we piled into two cars and headed for the lake. The boys drove Doug and Gerry and Jim. Gordie and I took the Dineens. It gave us a chance to renew our friendship, and to ask the questions that had been churning inside us.

Pat Dineen is a slight, pixylike woman with a husky voice, very Irish and with a real gleam in her eye. Bill has a kind of "Columbo" casualness. He's cool and unassuming and yet clever. In Houston the players called him "Foxy."

We spent a relaxing weekend, sailing and skiing and mixing the Houston group with our Bear Lake gang, a very special collection of friends. It wasn't a heavy-drinking bunch—we aren't that kind of crew—but we had fun putting on skits and barbecuing steaks, the kind of square things people did before they ran out of time. The Bear Lake regulars treated our Houston visitors as though we were all having a reunion.

When Jim Smith left he said, "These people can't be for real. I'm sure you rented them just to impress us."

We said our good-bys. Then Gordie and I went inside the cottage and sat down, instinctively, at the long black walnut table my dad had built. Gordie constructed the benches to match. Wherever we have lived, the kitchen table or whatever served as the kitchen table, has been the Howe meeting place. This was where we reached our most serious decisions and where we gravitated in idle moments to eat, play cards, work crosswords, begin projects, and drink hot tea by the gallon. Even though the kids always had their own desks, they ended up doing their algebra problems and term papers on the kitchen table.

I suspected that this went back to our own childhood days

on the farm, when the kitchen was the warmest spot in the house. Our kitchen tables have become family heirlooms. We'll never be able to sell them. Too much of our family life has been written on them.

At Bear Lake that day, Gordie and I sat down and started talking. We realized how garbled our emotions were. They tumbled out. It was one thing for the boys to sign with this new league, but what about Gordie? A Leo Durocher could cross the bridge from Brooklyn to New York. A John Connally could switch political parties. But Gordie had a reputation, one he cherished, as a player above vanity and greed. Would his fans think he had sold out?

Loyalties aside, there was the question of his health. That concerned me. Bill Dineen had spoken about using Gordie for spot appearances. I knew Gordie would have no part in that. He would not consent to be a once-a-week box office draw. The one thing Gordie had never learned, in twenty-five years of playing hockey, was to sit on the bench. He surely didn't intend to start learning now.

I glanced at my husband. He was still handsome, with hazel eyes that always held a hint of mischief and a mouth shaped for a grin. There were lots of scar traces, too—thin white lines that gave his face what artists call character. He really had changed little in all these years, but, I told myself, this was no time to get romantic. I didn't want him hurt or, worse than that, embarrassed.

Gordie had gained some weight around his middle. I would grab him by the midriff and pinch and say, "Hey, what's this?"

"That's my skating muscle," he'd say.

Gordie's "skating muscle" came not so much from being off the ice, but from attending too many banquets and sitting behind an empty desk with too little to do.

I also worried about the two other Howes — Murray and Cathy. Like his older brothers, Murray had been playing hockey even before he could see over the boards. At thirteen, he was playing as often as five times a week. We had a feeling, and Pat Dineen confirmed it, that there wasn't much in the way of amateur hockey in Houston. It just isn't an easy sport to play on sand. We didn't want to deny Murray the chance that his brothers had had to develop his own talent.

And Cathy, a pretty brown-haired Chris Evert type, reacted with horror at the thought of being uprooted and torn away from her friends in Detroit and being hauled off to Texas.

Before we made any final decisions, we realized we had better fly to Houston to see the town and get to know the Aeros owners. I had never been to Texas. For all I knew it was tumbleweed and cactus and oil wells growing in people's backyards.

You just don't devote yourself to one city and one association and then suddenly turn it off and walk away. It had been such a permanent thing that you really couldn't imagine someone named Gordie Howe not living in Detroit, not playing for the Red Wings. We worried about leaving all that. And we worried about the fans. Would they fault our sons for setting a precedent that could, according to some critics, hurt the junior hockey programs? But we still had to find out if the pluses in Texas would outweigh the minuses.

The moment our plane touched down, we were treated to a Texas welcome: limousine at the airport, yellow roses in the suite, our own nameplates on our doors at the Whitehall Hotel. They had even set a Coke bar in Murray's room.

That night we saw a baseball game at the Astrodome, then went to dinner with a party that included Paul Deneau, the original owner of the Aeros, who had flown down from his home in Dayton, Ohio, and two local investors, E. Z. Jones and Irvin Kaplan and their wives. Before the end of the next season, Kaplan, whose interests included banks and commercial real estate, had bought out Deneau.

We were impressed with all of them. E. Z. Jones was a dead

ringer for James Garner, tall and handsome, the classic Texan. Irv Kaplan was modest and businesslike, low-keyed. There comes a time when you have to put your trust in someone and ride out a decision. These were substantial people, the city was alive and friendly, and we made up our minds to put our careers—and our family—in their hands. That evening clinched it. We were going to Houston.

The papers hadn't been signed yet, but we had agreed to what would undoubtedly be the biggest family package in the history of sports—a little under the $2.5 million over four years that we had sought, but still an offer we couldn't refuse.

Only a few details remained to be settled. Gordie had promised me he would go to the hospital in Ann Arbor to get a complete physical checkup by Dr. Bob Bailey before we made it official. His state of health was now the major question for me. And the Aeros were signing a player forty-five years old, without even knowing if he had heart trouble. They never even asked.

Dr. Bailey put Gord through the entire series of tests. He even went behind his eyeballs to check for hardening of the arteries. He pronounced him in excellent health, told him to take off a few pounds, and said, "I've really got some bad news for you. Gordie, you're probably going to live to be a hundred and five. If you want to skate for the Aeros, you have my blessing."

Next came two phone calls that erased our last doubts. John Curran, a business partner and friend of our family, called to tell Gord he'd have a job waiting for him if the team or the league or the whole idea bombed out.

Then another friend, Chuck Robertson, the kind of guy who always seems to call and ask if he can help just when you are about to send up a flare, was on the phone. "If you're worried about Murray," he volunteered, "and you want him to continue with his hockey here, we'd love to have him. We'll care for him as if he were our own son."

Chuck is a lifelong hockey buff who owns a pool-construction business in Detroit. That's how we met. We were having a problem with our pool and Chuck came out himself, tripping over his feet at the idea of being inside Gordie Howe's home. Later, Murray played on one of the four minor hockey teams Chuck sponsored. He's a good-looking fellow in his early forties, with a beautiful wife, a son, and four daughters. He is genuine and generous and hard-working and has never stopped being our friend.

Everything, it seemed, had fallen into place for the Howes of Detroit to become the Howes of Houston. All that remained was for Gordie to give his notice to his employers of the last twenty-seven years. It had seemed, much of that time, to have been more than a player-team association. It had been a partnership, a romance. To more than one generation of fans, he *was* the Red Wings.

All that remained was one phone call to Bruce Norris.

2
Bitter Ice: Good-by, Detroit

THEY WERE WAITING in Texas for the signal from Gordie — an all clear to release the story. For two or three days I had nudged him as gently as I could; we were all sort of hanging from the chandelier.

By now rumors were epidemic in Detroit. Only five weeks had gone by since Doug Harvey's phone call had caught us going out the door, but they passed like freight cars at a railroad crossing. It seemed that we had wrestled with this decision forever.

On June 11, 1973, Gordie left the house for the Plum Hollow Country Club, just outside Detroit, where a golf tournament was held each year in his honor—the Gordie Howe Invitational. He said he would call Bruce Norris from the clubhouse before the tourney.

As soon as he finished the call to Bruce, he walked over to the first tee and told me. It was then I knew the Detroit part of our lives was over. I had a lump in my throat the size of a golf ball. I can only guess what it was like for Gordie.

Bruce Norris, the president of the Red Wings, was in his office when Gordie reached him. Bruce was one of those people who seemed to have been born behind a large glossy desk. He was tall, attractive, with thinning blond hair, reserved, dry, and little given to small talk. He was Gordie's age, the son of a remarkable man—Jim Norris—who lived in Chicago, once owned both the Black Hawks and the Red Wings, and helped build the National Hockey League. The older vendors and office help at the Olympia always spoke kindly of the senior Mr. Norris.

Few had worked for the Norris family any longer than Gordie. The late Jack Adams was running the club for them when the Red Wings brought Gordie out of the poverty of Saskatoon. In return, Gordie had filled the seats at the Olympia and helped establish Detroit as a power in the N.H.L.—he appeared in the playoffs nineteen times.

"Bruce," he said, when Norris answered, "I haven't signed with Houston yet. But I have made up my mind I won't be returning to the Olympia. It's not fair to you or the club to let this keep hanging on. I don't want this hassle to continue."

It was a short, pointed conversation. When Gordie put the receiver down he felt a wave of relief. He only vaguely remembered Bruce saying he was sorry it had all turned out like this.

Gordie announced his resignation that night to the press. He had never lied to them. He admitted that his last few years with the Red Wings hadn't been happy ones and that he was considering an offer from Houston to team up with his sons.

The Detroit papers had a field day, taking the Red Wings to task. The recent misadventures of the front office had created many critics, and Gordie's departure became a rallying point for them. The franchise had been in decline since 1967. The team had reached the playoffs only once during that time. Now all the attacks were in the open. Gordie's comments, which echoed with regret but were not vicious, still made good reading to those who had grown impatient with the team's management. The press dug up errors that had occurred over the years and old wounds were reopened.

It went on for a week, and then I received a phone call from John Ziegler, the attorney for Bruce Norris. "Colleen," he said, "we're very disappointed in Gordie. If he wants to leave, why can't he just go ahead and leave? Why is he trying to take the organization to task and tear it apart?"

Have you ever seen an Irish blonde with steam coming out of her ears? I blurted out, "If he wanted to hurt the club he probably could. But nothing Gordie has said or done was intended to hurt the Red Wings. Don't you understand? There are so many people unhappy with the Red Wings, they're using Gordie's decision as a way to get at the club.

"Yes, if Gordie goes to Houston, part of the reason is that he wasn't happy here. That's no secret. But the main reason is for the chance to play alongside his sons. He's a little bigger person than to make the Red Wings a goat. And anyone who doesn't know that, doesn't know Gordie Howe."

I felt frustrated when I hung up the phone. It was like trying to move a ten-ton marshmallow from your driveway. You can kick all you want but it won't budge. It was typical of Gordie's recent years with the club that Bruce Norris had felt it necessary to go through a third party. Gordie finally wrote him a letter, just a few polite paragraphs, saying that he hoped someday they could sit down, just the two of them, and let Gordie explain some of the things he felt.

Within hours after Gordie had called to say he was resigning, his secretary, Dorothy Ringler, was fired.

For what it was worth, no one really tried very hard to dissuade him from leaving the Red Wings. A couple of phone calls had been made with backhanded offers, including one from Bruce.

"Gordie, this is going to be my last offer," he said. "You can also have a P.R. job with the league and they'll match your salary here." In the same breath he added, "But you'll have to do a helluva lot more work than you've been doing for us."

For two years Gordie had complained to anyone who would listen, Norris included, that he was in a nonjob and felt useless. Now it was being suggested that he had been a goldbrick.

We knew the important thing was not to lose our composure. If you feel yourself drowning, struggling only speeds up the process. Gordie was determined to leave in a way that would make it possible for him to feel welcome if he ever walked back into the Olympia. He wanted to be able to show his grandchildren through there someday and tell them, "This is where I spent most of my life."

So Gordie and I went to the arena to say good-by to anyone who wanted to say good-by to us. It was a parting, we decided, but it needn't be a grim one. And there in the hallway we bumped head-on into Ned Harkness, the Detroit general manager, who had taken much of the brunt of Gordie's leaving, something we regretted very much.

He was a decent man who had been only indirectly involved with Gordie's problems. Ned was so intense he had a difficult time relating to people. He was a person who listened hard and never heard what you said.

Ned was the strong, physical type, with rugged good looks, the type who would go into a losing locker room and wish he could put his fist through the wall. He used the *famous* four-letter word so often in his locker room talks, Gordie complained that he couldn't concentrate on what Ned was saying. He just found himself counting the number of times he said *the word*.

But no one ever tried harder. He had succeeded Sid Abel as coach in 1970 and was so unpopular with the fans, his family had to stop coming to the games. The players held a private meeting to try to have him fired, and eventually he was moved upstairs to the general manager's job. It was a pity because Ned Harkness would have crawled through fire to produce a winning team.

We were suddenly face to face with Ned, and he was shaking with emotion. He had never been particularly close to Gordie, but he was near tears. "Gord," he said, "I've offered my job back to Bruce Norris, if you'll stay."

There are rare human moments in sports that touch you deeply. But Gordie told Ned, gently, that the decision was behind us and we were ready to look ahead now. We said good-by. It was too late for explanations.

Management's parting words would come in a less personal way. We had already heard from Dorothy Ringler how the vultures descended on Gordie's office immediately after he resigned. The place looked like a Sunday flea market, she said, with people grabbing chairs, filing cabinets, and waste baskets.

Our final good-by was in the form of Gordie's last pay check, which normally ran a little over $2,000. This one was for $50. The Red Wings had deducted from his salary our last month's bill with the Olympia Travel Bureau, which Bruce Norris owned. We automatically booked any flying we or the children did through the agency. And we paid our bills promptly.

To Gordie, it was an unbelievable putdown. Apparently, someone didn't think his word or his credit was reliable. The pay-check incident did one thing for me. If I had any lingering regret, or nostalgia, about leaving the Red Wings, that wiped it out. It was strictly business.

Gordie's leave-taking was not unique in professional sports. There is often pettiness or meanness, and bitter words on one side or the other—often both—when a player is traded or released. When he plays out his contract or jumps leagues those emotions multiply. It gets personal because sports, unlike fields where people work with stocks or flowers or meat, *is* so personal and so public.

I remember reading once that Vince Lombardi, the football coach, cried when he let a favorite player, Paul Hornung, go in an expansion draft (but he *did* let him go). On the other hand, another player, Jim Taylor, played out his option and made a deal with the same team that wound up with Hornung, and Lombardi never again *mentioned* his name.

In Gordie's case, he was the superstar athlete to whom ownership over the years had made a series of vague promises about business connections and a front-office future. "You're going to help us run the club," they assured him. But no one bothered to train him, and seldom were the promises remembered.

For two years I had watched my husband languish in an office so tacky that whenever the Red Wings needed a promotional picture, they moved him into someone else's office. We laughed because the "front office" shots always showed pictures of someone else's kids hanging in the background. There are a lot of small ways to make people feel nonessential.

I don't doubt that there were good intentions, at least in the beginning. Bruce Norris wanted Gordie in the Red Wings' organization. The problem was that none of Bruce's people could decide what Gordie was supposed to be doing. Maybe they expected him to sit in that office and leaf through his old scrapbooks. Gordie wasn't any better at chairwarming than he was at benchwarming.

The job became a source of embarrassment. He literally didn't know what to say when people asked him what he did.

Meanwhile, he had renewed his state life-insurance license. Repeatedly, he was led to believe that he would have a position, an interest, a directorship, in one of the Norris insurance companies. He kept thinking he was going into some kind of executive training program. People were always going to call him back in a few days, and nothing ever happened.

It all could have been so simple. Gordie wanted to contribute, and if the Red Wings organization had found a way to let him, had shown that they cared about Gordie Howe,

Houston might never have seen us. Mark and Marty might have gone on to the new league without their dad, but we'll never know about that, either.

The bitterness in which we left Detroit brought back an unpleasant memory of my first meeting with Bruce Norris, which I had long since tried to forget. This occurred at an annual year-end party the Norrises always gave for the team. The Red Wings had lost in the playoffs, but it was a lovely party nevertheless.

As the night wore on, and the booze kept flowing, Gordie said, "Let's go before all the year-end hostilities start coming out. I'll get our coats." I told Gord I would first thank our host for the party.

I walked over and said, "Mr. Norris, I know how disappointed you are that the team lost. And I appreciate the lovely party you gave for them."

Bruce fixed me with a narrowed eye and proceeded to light into me with a vengeance. He began by roaring that I didn't deserve a guy like Gordie. He said he knew about my "ski trips" and was aware of my "affairs."

Tears started rolling down my cheeks. I stood there, stunned. I ran out of the room and burst into tears in the hallway. I couldn't even quit sobbing long enough to tell Gordie what was wrong. By the time I did we were home, and Gord went to the phone, called Jack Adams, the coach, and said, "Jack, I have played my last game for the Red Wings."

I no longer remember what year that was, or which team we lost to in the playoffs. The years all run together. I only remember that it was the kind of hurt that lasts a lifetime, and it was at least fifteen years before Gordie really did play his last game for the Red Wings.

Team parties can be explosive. Some have cost teams a title. Some lead to fights and others turn into all-night songfests at a piano bar. Still others just leave scars that are not soon forgotten.

This was in a less-sophisticated time, when married women whose husbands traveled were in a very difficult position. It was like being married to a prisoner of war. I wasn't the type to sit at home and watch "I Love Lucy" on TV. I went skiing on weekends with the children and with other couples. I sometimes went to cocktail parties and weddings alone, and people gossiped. People love to gossip. But nothing I had done could have given Bruce Norris a reason for saying the things he said to me that night.

Bruce woke up the next morning and didn't remember any of it. He wrote a personal note of apology and sent a gift, a camera. A sincere apology would have been adequate. The gift wasn't necessary nor was it appreciated. But I wrote him back and said I, too, was sorry it had happened, and I intended to forget the incident even though I didn't know what I had done to deserve it.

The incident was difficult to put behind me, though I really tried to forget it. Gordie was now an established star with most of his career in front of him, and I wanted him to do well in Detroit. But some tension always remained between me and the man who employed my husband.

Bruce had great affection for Gordie in the way that men in sports often have for a player whose talent is special. I'm sure I was resented by some people close to the team. I never hesitated to speak out when I saw something that I felt was wrong, or could be improved. This typed me as a *pushy, interfering wife.*

I was around the Olympia more than the other wives because, for one thing, I had established the junior hockey program there. I was always displeased—and said so—that the arena was seldom kept clean. I thought it wrong to make the fans—the team's bread and butter—sit on filthy seats. My opinions rubbed many people, including possibly Bruce Norris, the wrong way.

At one point Gordie was trying to clear up some of the

confusion about the insurance job, and explain his problem in the front office. He insisted on meeting Bruce in Miami, where he kept a residence. For obvious reasons I felt it best to stay home, but Gordie insisted that I go with him.

The W.H.A. was just a seedling then. Gordie wasn't thinking about defecting, he just wanted to clear the air. Bruce could not have been more cordial. He assured Gordie everything would be worked out. He thanked me for my efforts on behalf of junior hockey and told me to think of the Olympia as though it were my own building.

We both felt pleased and exalted when we left Bruce's apartment. It was great what could be accomplished when mature people sat down and talked frankly. The world was a good place, after all. Gordie was loved and I, Colleen, was at least tolerated.

At the airport Gordie was paged, to our surprise, since no one knew we had left Detroit. Howard Erikson, a Detroit *Free Press* reporter, was calling, asking why he was in Miami. Gordie, as always, told the truth—that he had met with Bruce Norris to work out some minor problems. Unfortunately, we didn't know the reporter had already talked to Bruce, who denied we were there.

We returned home and Gordie went right back to his job as a banquet attraction. He felt insecure, even an outsider—an odd comment to make after twenty-seven years with one team. He went to league meetings, but if he was asked for an opinion his advice was never taken. Finally, he quit going.

He had good reason to feel insecure. All around us people were being released. There was so much upheaval in Detroit that even if you were told you had a lifetime job, you didn't run out and plant a sequoia tree.

In retrospect, the low point of Gordie's Detroit career didn't involve him. It was the firing, in 1966, of Bill Gadsby as coach. Gordie had played hockey with and against Bill for many years and his wife, Edna, is my closest friend.

To this day Bill carries the scars of hockey, but they lend character to a face that women would describe as "interesting." Edna is slight, with dark eyes and hair and classic features. Her instincts are gentle, but at times she can be the Rock of Gibraltar. The Gadsbys have four daughters and it's a loving family.

Bill was in Edmonton working in junior hockey when the Red Wings called and offered him the coaching job. The first thing he did was call Gordie and say, "Look, if you want that job when you retire, I won't take it." He is that kind of man. Gordie urged him to take it.

The Red Wings were slipping when Bill arrived, and there was a lot of flack and uneasiness during his first year. At times he doubted he would be back for a second season. But he was. The team won its first three games during the second season. Then, suddenly, he was fired.

Edna and I met in the hallway in the Olympia before the game that night, neither of us aware of what had already happened. I took her down to the insurance office on the ground floor to introduce her to some friends there. The head of the agency called me into his office and said, "You ought to know that Bill Gadsby has just been fired."

I don't think he had any idea what kind of impact that news would have on me. Edna and I walked out of there, and my mind was spinning. I knew I owed it to her to tell her—yet it wasn't my place. What if the report wasn't correct? So I said, "Edna, someone said Bill is trying to find you. I think we'd better go look for him. He'll never be able to track us down."

When we spotted Bill I could tell by the look on his face the news was true. I said, "Edna, Bill has something to tell you. I'll leave the two of you alone."

They went upstairs to talk. After a few minutes I followed them. I knew she would need a friend.

I dreaded to think what a jolt this had to be. They had sold their home, uprooted everything in Edmonton, and then Bill was fired after three wins in his second season with the Red Wings. I found Edna in the ladies room, crying. She couldn't understand why it had happened. She was concerned about her family, how they would cope, but more than that she hurt for Bill as only a wife can hurt.

Bill never did find out why he had been fired. They gave him vague excuses, said he "lacked sophistication," but provided no real explanation. The Detroit club covered its flanks well. A clause in Bill's letter of release stipulated that if he made any critical remarks to the press his pay would be cut off immediately. He had a family to feed and a mortgage to pay. He went out as they wanted him to—quietly.

Whatever innocence Gordie had left about his sport, he lost most of it when Bill Gadsby was fired. Looking back, we should have seen a little of what was in store for us.

During his last two years in Detroit, I saw the flame that had always been in Gordie slowly fade. By nature an "up" person, he was now constantly down, and not entirely because he loathed going to the office.

Simply, Gordie missed being on the team, sharing the camaraderie among the players on the flights and in the locker room. He would go down to visit with the guys, but it just wasn't the same. When you are part of a team you all move in the same orbit; you eat, drink, and practically breathe together. The humor is all off the wall, very inside, and if you aren't around all the time you just can't be a part of it, no matter how close you once were. The players don't intentionally leave you out. But somebody makes a crack and everybody laughs. Most of the time Gordie didn't know what they were laughing about. As a result, he would come home more depressed than when he left.

My only regret was that we didn't leave sooner. Maybe twenty-seven years was too long to spend with any one club or organization. You learn from any experience, good or bad, but I know that at least two of those years were wasted.

But it was time to forget the past—except, of course, the sweet nights and friendly people, all the winning scoreboards, and the goals that went in. We'd always have that, and Gordie's sweet success. Now, however, it was time to start thinking about the boys, Mark and Marty, our move to Texas, and the second coming of Gordie Howe.

In the weeks before we left Detroit, in every interview they gave, on whatever show they appeared, Gordie and the boys talked about the opportunity of a lifetime awaiting us in Houston. There were no recriminations, no talk about the sorrows and the hurts. We didn't want to thumb our noses at the Red Wings.

Calls and letters poured in from the Midwest and Canada, from fans who said they couldn't wait to see Number Nine back on the ice. Only a few made comments like, "What are you trying to do? Cash in on your sons' talents?" We'd have to see about that.

We still felt a twinge that the boys hadn't been given a chance to turn pro with the National Hockey League. (The age requirement was lifted a year later.) But they were ready to test themselves, and I watched proudly as they handled the pressure already coming their way.

When a reporter asked them how it would feel to be playing alongside their famous father, Mark said softly, "I doubt that I'll be playing that much. I'll probably be on the bench cheering for him . . . *just like always.*"

Three months of uncertainty, aches, pains, confusion, the relocation blues, and occasional panic went by. But I knew it would all be worthwhile—that we had made the right decision—the night I saw Gordie, Mark, and Marty Howe create history as the first father-son teammates in professional sports. It was October 1973, and I almost pinched myself as I sat in the stands of the old Sam Houston Coliseum, and saw them skate onto the ice for their first home game with the Houston Aeros.

It couldn't be true. Too many cards had been stacked against the Howes. But there they were, the three of them. Gord's hair was grayer, thinner, his middle only slightly paunchy after six hard weeks of going through a physical conditioning regimen in camp. But how familiar those long, strong, Popeye-sized arms looked with a hockey stick in grips again.

I don't know how many true hockey nuts were in the Texas crowd that night, but they surely couldn't mistake one sight: the Gordie Howe skate. I can't describe it, except to say it's computer fast, effortless, and as graceful to watch as any figure skater I've ever seen. It is as distinctive as Musial's wiggle at the plate, a style all Gordie's own, unlike any other hockey player.

The Number Nine jumped out at me—but how different, how strange Gordie looked in blue. Later he said, "When I looked down for the first time and saw that blue uniform, I felt like I had my skates on the wrong feet."

Marty and Mark looked very boyish to me, like the teen-agers they were. They had that excited, here-we-go look that can be glimpsed in the eye of every rookie who ever played the game.

As I fidgeted with my program, waiting for the game to start, I realized what a toll the last few months had taken—how tired and worried I was. A friend had brought us a case of Coors beer to help ease the pain of unpacking. We were still moving into our new two-story home, the one whose closets, Gordie boasted, "were bigger than the bedrooms we had back in Detroit." Boxes were still piled everywhere. But I hadn't the energy or the heart or the time to empty them. Two planeloads of Detroit friends and a squadron of out-of-state press had flown in the day before the game.

E. Z. Jones, one of the part-owners of the Aeros, had

arranged for a genuine Texas *howdy*, with western string-tie band and cowgirls, and a police escort into town. I was there to greet them with the cheerless news that Gordie was in the hospital and might not appear in the opening game.

He had injured his back during the Aeros' preseason tour. Slowly but surely, the spasms started setting in. Then he made the mistake of skating with the team for a promotion at a place called the Galleria. The Galleria is Houston's version of Rockefeller Center, except the ice rink is indoors and surrounded by three stories of shops, where you can buy everything from a Tiffany diamond to a Neiman-Marcus fur.

Gord had no business being there, much less skating, but he was never one to baby pain. The following morning he couldn't get out of bed. I called the Aeros' team physician, who promptly admitted him to Sharpstown General Hospital and put him in traction. I was heartsick. Not only had I mentally written off the opener, but it was a dismal and discouraging way to begin our Houston experience.

The next day, the morning of the game, Gordie called from the hospital and said he was coming home for a pre–game meal. "I'm going to at least try to dress out and play a shift," he said.

I told him he was crazy, that he was doing this to annoy me, and if he came to the game at all I would pretend I didn't know him.

Sure enough, there he was flicking the puck around, warming up to take on the Cleveland Crusaders. On the way to the game, I had driven past a skyscraper draped with a huge banner that read, WELCOME TO HOWESTON. But I was so worried about Gordie's back that I couldn't enjoy the warm gestures or the pregame ceremonies.

I did notice a number of fans were disguising themselves as empty seats. I later learned that Houston fans, unlike their counterparts to the north, seldom arrive more than a half-hour before game time. Often, the puck drops before they do.

I also decided that the Aeros—and the Howes—had quite a P.R. job ahead of them.

The Sam Houston Coliseum was a tourist attraction in its heyday, which was a few years after World War I. It seated only 9,600, and by face-off time it was two-thirds full.

My mind kept coming back to Gordie. Could he play the kind of hockey that would make him feel proud? Should he be out there at all? I knew he would never be satisfied to merely be acceptable. Gordie had said, "If I go out there and make a fool of myself, that is all they'll remember. They might forget everything else I did."

And what if some rookie decided to make a name for himself by taking a cheap shot at a Hall-of-Famer and injured him seriously? I thought about the boys. Mark had been compared to Bobby Hull, Marty to a budding Bobby Orr. Both had been outstanding in junior hockey. But this was the pros, and they had a big name and a big salary they had to justify.

As these thoughts splashed through my mind, I noticed something that cracked me up and, blessedly, broke the tension. Marty tapped his dad on the shoulder as they headed onto the ice. He pointed to Gord's back. I could see him straining to look over his shoulder.

There for all the world to see—only the press missed it—was his first name misspelled. How ironic. A superstar makes a monumental return to the ice and has to skate the entire game with G-O-R-I-D-E blocked out on the back of his jersey.

The game against Cleveland remains a blur. I remember thinking that Gord and his sons played an outstanding game, but I was crushed that the Aeros lost. And I was puzzled, as Mark and Marty were, when the crowd gave them a standing ovation as they left the ice.

Mark was at his father's elbow. "Don't they know we lost?" the mixed-up rookie asked. And the mixed-up veteran just shrugged.

It was true that not all of them understood the game. Texas, we knew, was football—not hockey—country. But I think they had seen something they liked. They saw a team in a new (to them) and exciting sport give its all. Texans set a heavy store by effort.

But there was something else—a sensation I had never experienced before, not on all those great and glorious nights when Gordie Howe was leading the Red Wings into championship games and scoring his 500th goal, and his 600th, and 700th. There was just this quality in the applause that night, when they stood and cheered a losing team, that seemed to say, "Welcome, Gordie and Mark and Marty. We may not understand your game, but we know a hero when we see one."

I had the feeling that hockey would do all right here in the heart of the oil and cattle belt. And so would the Howes. For the moment, at least, Detroit was forgotten.

A few weeks later, some of our friends in Miami ran into Bruce Norris. I was anxious to hear what he had said to them. We wanted the bitter feelings to be gone. I had saved a Red Wing souvenir program that celebrated Gordie's twenty-fifth season with the club, and in it Bruce had written an open letter. He listed Gordie's achievements, mentioned his personal regard for this "great guy," and wished him twenty-five more years with the Red Wings.

Our friends introduced themselves and said, "We know a gentleman-friend of yours in Houston. "

And Bruce Norris said, "I have no gentleman-friend in Houston. "

3
That Championship Season

NOT LONG AFTER the Howes had settled in Houston, we were running some old hockey films at a booster club meeting, films I hadn't seen in years. Then, suddenly, on the screen was Jack Adams, Gordie's old coach who had discovered him for the Red Wings, and he was saying something that gave me goose bumps.

Jack described the big, rough, unschooled, unpolished kid he had first observed as a sixteen-year-old at a Windsor tryout camp. Then he laughed, and said, "Gordie spoke so slowly, he sounded like a *Texan.*"

It was so ironic, so strange. Of course, Gordie was a Canadian. I was born across the border, in Detroit. But we discovered quickly how much they had in common—Texas and Canada: the bigness, the richness, the openness, the try-anything spirit, the warmth of the people. I guess there has always been this affinity. Before the war, *our* war, the second one, Texans had flocked in surprising number to join the Royal Canadian Air Force, impatient for the United States to join the shooting.

So here we were, transplanted Texans, as so many of them are. Back in Detroit, our friends and Gordie's fans talked about our leaving, not as a move to a new city and new jobs, but as though it were a political exile. It had been "hot copy" in the press for weeks, argued about in every bar and barber shop in the city. We were swamped with best wishes by mail and a series of farewell parties where I cried my eyes out every night.

And then, Texas.

Let us suppose that you had decided to write a movie script about an aging, former hockey great who comes out of retirement to play on the same team with two of his sons, both in their teens. You make the locale a city where, in the summer, the heat reduces your brain to the size and texture of a smoked oyster. The old man finds his touch, wins the Most Valuable Player award, and the younger son is voted Rookie of the Year. For a big finish, you have the team win the league championship.

Hollywood would never buy it.

There just aren't many cornball stories like that anymore. And it was exactly what we had ahead of us, down to the last win over Chicago for the AVCO Trophy and the champagne shower in the locker room on the last night of the season. You don't daydream on that kind of scale. You don't even pray for it. My observation has been that pro athletes go into a new season with just one real ambition: not to screw up.

Gordie and the boys had some adjusting to do. Realistically we knew football was king in Texas and that most of the fans thought of ice as something to keep their maraschino cherries cold in a tall glass. Blue lines and faceoffs just weren't in the Texas vocabulary. A lot of people seemed to be having a good deal of fun at the novelty of hockey in the tropics. It was like holding a rodeo on the beach of Waikiki.

A Toronto newspaper sent a reporter down to Houston to report on the Howes' reception, and he went back with a tongue-in-cheek, man-on-the-street report. One Houstonian thought Gordie Howe was a rock star, but he wasn't sure about the identity of the group to which he belonged. A parking-lot attendant swore he was a golfer. A geologist couldn't quite make up his mind, but he believed Gord had something to do with South Africa. When the reporter did find a fan who had heard of him, the comment was, "Yeah, a guy like Howe can really put that little ol' black ball in the cage."

While the Howes weren't totally convinced of the validity of random surveys, we did get the message. Especially Gordie. A few days after his arrival, he dropped by the offices of the Aeros to see Jim Smith. He introduced himself to the young lady at the reception desk.

"Hi. I'm Gordie Howe. To see Jim Smith."

She looked at him blankly. "May I say what it's in reference to?" she asked, reaching for the intercom button.

Gordie resisted the temptation to say that it was in reference to the rising cost of nutmeg. When he returned home that day he said, "I think I'd better start spending some time around the Aeros' offices, so the secretaries will know I work there."

Clearly, the Houston ice-hockey team needed promoting, and Gordie and the boys were prepared to do whatever was required—with one exception. Gord drew the line at riding an elephant.

The year before, when the World Hockey Association was still a debutante and the Aeros were desperate to get their name in the paper, the publicity man, Sonny Tate, talked Bill Dineen into riding an elephant through downtown in the annual Shrine Circus parade. Bill, nice guy that he is, dutifully climbed onto the back of an elderly, sleepy mastodon and went wobbling along the parade route, looking like a pale, spastic Gunga Din.

He was just beginning to get his mouth to work again, trying to form a smile, when his elephant decided to make friends with him. I'm afraid there is no delicate way to say this. The elephant in front of them relieved himself, whereupon Bill's leaned down, snorted up the entire puddle with his trunk, curled the trunk back over his head, and sprayed the coach of the Houston Aeros. Never let it be said that Bill Dineen didn't give his all for ice hockey.

But Gordie Howe wasn't that brave, and neither were his sons. They let Sonny Tate know that if he ever needed an elephant rider, to be sure and look somewhere else.

We moved into our new home less than a month before the season was scheduled to open, and even the movers who were unloading huge boxes filled with N.H.L. trophies didn't know who we were. They thought Mark, who had pitched in, did our yard work or something.

Tired and out of sorts, Mark finally said, "Look, I'm Mark Howe. I play hockey. I *live* here."

We were trying to beat a storm, so Gordie and the boys were helping with the muscle work. Hurricane Delia was threatening to hit the Gulf Coast. The sky was darkening and there was an odd smell of wet flannel in the air.

It was all new to us. Ice storms we could handle, but hurricanes were another, strange form of Mother Nature running amuck. Luckily, when the storm came, only the fringe of it hit Houston.

We had bought a new home in the Memorial section of the city, an affluent area where many oil-company executives and doctors live. I had left Detroit with visions of finding only adobe-style houses, but I was amazed at all the traditional and colonial ones. They didn't have the cellars or basements to which we were accustomed in the north—flooding was a problem in Houston, which is flat as a pool table.

Gordie was positively fascinated with the neighborhood. I think he drove every reporter and every friend who came to town past one particular house a few blocks away. In their *yard* they had two horses, two Texas longhorn steers, and two buffalo. He just couldn't get over it.

"Can you believe it?" he would say to his passengers, slowing down. "Right here in the middle of a city." Gordie cruised by there so many times, I'm sure those neighbors thought they were being cased for a burglary.

Except for the occasional thrill of discovery, those first few days and weeks were horrendous. We were five basket cases. The boys drove down from Detroit, and on the way our family pup, Skippy, suffered a heat stroke in a small town in Arkansas. The boys had left him in the car for only twenty minutes, while they went inside a cafe to eat, but that apparently was too long under a midday Arkansas sun. The town had no vet and the local hospital turned them away. In desperation, they rushed back to the cafe and put the pup under the faucet in the rest room until the running water revived him.

Skippy didn't travel well, and now I wasn't too sure about the rest of us. Boxes nearly reached the ceiling, new furniture was weeks late in arriving, and the yard wasn't yet landscaped—it didn't seem much like home.

Cathy and I gulped McDonald's hamburgers and kept moving as quickly as possible. Gordie and the boys were gone through most of what I had come to think of as *my* ordeal. They were on a whirlwind promotion tour for the league, traveling to New York, Toronto, and Montreal while we unpacked.

Cathy, who would be fifteen in six months, if I let her live, detested Houston, swore she would never change her opinion, and begged to return to Detroit. I remember sitting on those boxes one day, not knowing where to begin, and thinking, "Why did we do this? It's insane."

As the personal things—the familiar lamps and chairs and mounted fish and trophies—came out of the boxes, the house began to look like something that belonged to the Howes.

Cathy continued to come home each day from school, go to her room and cry. I tried giving her sympathy. I knew it was difficult at her age. But I was having problems, too. So many times we had come close to changing our minds about letting Murray stay behind. He was the youngest, the baby. What if he found out he didn't need a mother?

Finally, I marched into Cathy's room and planted my feet. "Look," I said, "I feel like crying, too. This is not easy for any of us, but we are only making it hard on each other. Now I want to see you snap out of it."

As a rule, Cathy abounds with energy. She loves people. She's artistic and athletic. She's the only brunette in the family, very pretty, with chocolate brown eyes that look like M & Ms. She loves to be involved in whatever is going on. Cathy is so concerned about people that we call her the Ann Landers of the Howe family.

Not long after that, four adorable teen-age guys in tennis outfits rang the front doorbell and asked if Cathy was home. That ended the crying spells. Everything was going to be fine, after all.

For nearly six weeks we had television crews and writers at our door, on our sofas, and under our feet. By the fifteenth of September, the Aeros were holding two-a-day workouts at a suburban rink called the Ice Haus. The Howes would practice in the morning, race home for an interview or taping, grab a bite to eat, and go back for the afternoon drill.

Sometimes CBS or a Canadian television crew would be waiting for them when they returned home for supper. I was delighted at the poise with which Mark and Marty continued to handle the attention. It was hard to come home exhausted after a double practice session and have the lights thrown on you for two hours while people dished out tough and sometimes repetitive questions. But these were major interviews, important to us and to the club.

We knew after the first six weeks that the Aeros and the

press would have what they wanted, if the Howes could last. A couple of times Marty walked in the door and grumbled, "Oh God, can't we just come home *one* day when there isn't somebody here?"

Gordie, of course, was geared to all this tumult. It was second nature to him. He had never balked at giving interviews, had an easy rapport with the press, and never wearied of telling the same when-did-you-get-your-first-skates story a hundred times over. We turned down many dinner and social invitations those first few weeks. I wanted the evenings quiet, so the hockey players could just flop into bed if they wanted.

Physically, Gordie was dragging. It had to be torture, trying to come back after a two-year layoff at going-on-forty-six. He would sag into the nearest chair and say, "Boy, I was blowing out there today. I was tripping all over myself. Couldn't even remember how to grab the stick."

It was pure drudgery, as he fought to lose twelve pounds and regain his rhythm, his touch. He would come home and fall into such a deep sleep that I felt guilty waking him for dinner. The practices were strenuous for a player of any age; can you imagine what they must have been like for one they had been calling The Old Man for ten years?

One night Mark came home, frowning. "Dad's face got red as a beet," he said. "I thought he was going to have a heart attack." My son's choice of words nearly gave me one. Mark and Marty both worried about Gordie and, I suspect, watched him very closely during those first days.

Finally I told Gord, "You know, you're the one who has to say. If it's too much, it's too much."

He looked at me, raised an eyebrow, but said nothing.

Through all the years, I had never seen him *really* despondent, not over an injury or a scoring slump or even a narrow loss. He had a tremendous capacity to absorb almost every kind of experience. When he was down, he would always be the first fellow on the ice the next day at practice. But I could tell Gordie was beginning to get apprehensive.

He wasn't terribly out-of-shape. He had never been a phys-ed freak, he didn't roll out of bed in the morning and jog three miles in his underwear. But he did do push-ups, watched his diet, didn't smoke, drank moderately, got his rest, and did some running. At the lake, he always ran the seventy-four steps—he counted them—that led from our cottage to the water.

But the sessions were brutal for him, even the primary stuff —the general skating and puck-handling drills. He puffed his way through them. I knew he needed more time to get his legs back. And he was worried about the wrist. He had been a one-handed player that last season with the Red Wings.

Training camp is always a trial for the veterans. The first week the rookies are whizzing right by you. The second week you're even with them. And the third, you're setting the pace and they follow. Gordie always picked out the fastest and best skater on the club and paced himself with that player. Gradually, he began to feel like himself again. He was an actor suddenly remembering lines from an old play.

Although it was mostly unspoken, we had another concern in the back of our minds. How would the other fellows react to a middle-aged geezer skating with them? It would not have been surprising for some to think, "Sure, he was good in his day. But what can he do now? The whole thing is a P. R. job." And the boys. Would the other players resent them and their salaries?

Hockey players are often strange, wild men with missing teeth who talk about their pain as though it were a hobby. But in matters that count I have found they can be big. There was no hint of animosity, no wall between the others and the Howes. They praised Gord, made him feel wanted and respected and needed. Never for a moment did he feel ill-at-ease with these new Aeros, many of whom were close to the ages of his sons.

I guess the team's goalie, Smokey McLeod, a veteran who had been a rookie years before in Detroit, said it for all of them. "Everyone knows what kind of a player Gordie Howe has been. You can't be jealous of Gordie Howe."

In a way, they were eager to see the legend perform. Smokey had been on the Red Wings' bench when Gordie was winding up his career. He hadn't forgotten a game against Toronto when a rookie, Jim Dorey, took Gordie into the boards, gave him an elbow, and worked him over. When his shift left the ice, Gordie came over to the bench and sat beside the young goalie.

"He has a funny habit," Smokey said. "He never uses his glove to wipe off the sweat like the other fellows. He just leans over and wipes his forehead on the shoulder of whoever is sitting next to him. He did it to me and I thought to myself, 'What's this? '

"But Gordie's mind was still out on the ice. He said, 'You know, Smokey, these rookies *never* learn.' The next shift he went into the corner with Dorey, and I was watching, see, because I *knew* Gordie was going to get even. The next thing I knew Gordie was skating away and Dorey was coming out, blood dripping from a cut across his forehead. I was watching, I didn't take my eyes off him, and I never saw it."

About the boys, the players were less respectful, but they were willing to judge them on how they produced, and that was all Mark and Marty asked. But all three had the preseason jitters. They felt they were under a microscope. They were either too young or too old, and the Howes had things to prove.

When they left for the first exhibition series on the road, Gordie said, "If I get through this trip I think I'm going to make it."

The preseason opener was in New York's famed Madison Square Garden, ironically, where Gordie had played his last game in the National Hockey League. The opponents were the Winnipeg Jets, featuring his foe of old, Bobby Hull. It was a match-up of two of the three most famous names ever to wear the Number Nine. Only the Rocket, Maurice Richard, was missing. Sonny Tate, the Aeros' publicist, had teasingly promised that the Rocket would be there to drop the puck, but that was one publicity stunt Sonny couldn't deliver.

Actually, Gordie had bumped the Number Nine off Mark's back to retrieve it for himself again. It had been Mark's number in amateur hockey, and it would be his again when his father retired. Gordie had a long talk about it with Marty who, as the eldest son, might have had a prior claim. It was no big deal, but the press was curious.

"Marty is a thin-skinned guy," Gordie explained, "but you can't hurt Mark's feelings. So I figured Mark would be better equipped to handle whatever abuse or attention went with wearing my number."

Marty didn't mind. "I'll make my own number," he said, with a grin.

Of course, Murray also wore Nine on his teams in Detroit. It seemed that whenever one of the Howe brothers went out for a team, the coach automatically assigned them *that* number. I don't recall it ever causing a problem among them.

Gordie wasted little time showing the world that the *real* Number Nine was out of mothballs. Just twenty-one seconds into his first shift on the ice he scored on a pass from Mark. Boy, I needed that. It had suddenly dawned on me that I was going to be more alone than ever, after having Gordie at home for two years. Now he and the boys would all be gone when the team traveled. I had also noticed that most of the players' wives were the ages of Mark and Marty.

I suddenly felt like the Queen Mother. So that goal gave me a glimpse of the good things ahead, and it did wonders for

Mom's spirit. The Aeros defeated the Jets, and although exhibition games are notoriously poor indicators of the coming season, it was a happy return for Gord.

The touring Aeros wended their way to Detroit—a piece of last-minute scheduling designed to milk the most out of off-season events. Gordie had gotten back to the Motor City sooner than he ever dreamed. When he glided onto the ice the sellout crowd stood as one and exploded with applause. I thought they would never stop. The ovation must have lasted five minutes as Gordie, grinning sheepishly, skated in small, aimless circles. There was a lot of love in that arena. The game between two World Hockey teams the crowd knew nothing about didn't really matter.

When we flew out of Detroit the next morning, Gordie turned in his seat and winked at me. "I'm going to make it," he said. If he hadn't believed that, there is no doubt in my mind he would have told the Aeros, "Look, I made a mistake," and put his skates back on the shelf.

Then, almost as if no one had been counting, the days were gone, it was opening night, and the season had gotten under way. With each game I could see everyone gaining momentum—Gordie, the boys, the team, the fans. The Old Man was having fun. He was back to acting like a big kid again. Gordie would skate over to the rail during practice or before a game and motion to a writer or someone from the Aeros' front office. "Have you ever seen anything like that?" he'd ask, holding up the flat side of his stick.

As the victim would lean down for a closer look, Gordie would give a flick of the blade and a half pound of ice shavings would pour into the guy's ear. He was remarkably adroit at that. It was one of his famous pranks, and to me it was a sign that he was returning to form.

Gordie and the boys were experiencing something unique among professional athletes—father and son teammates sharing the same locker room, going on the same road trips.

At first it startled me to hear the boys calling their father "Gordie." But I understood. It would have sounded silly on the ice for them to be yelling "Dad."

He was no chaperone on the road, but the ingredients must have been there for a nice situation comedy—rated PG, of course (parental guidance recommended). I would have loved to have been invisible or hiding in a closet to see how they handled it.

Marty, I think, was always more inclined to be on his own. But Mark would come up to his father and say, "Are you having dinner with anyone tonight, Dad?"

There is some natural separation on any team into the marrieds, the nonmarrieds, and what Mark and Marty called the might-as-well-be married guys. And, of course, I knew the three of them were taking a fearful kidding from the other players.

In the locker room, one of them would yell, "Hey, Marty, who are you going out with tonight? Has she got a mother for Gordie?" Everyone would roar. Locker-room humor seldom goes over anyone's head.

I suppose it was a curious situation in which all three found themselves. If the boys were going out drinking and had in mind meeting some girls and stirring up a little romance, do they tell their father? Or ask him to come along?

In the dressing room and on the ice, they tried mightily to be three hockey players doing their job. Some of the fans ran the dad business into the ground early in the season. If Mark complained to a referee, or skated in the direction of Gordie, the yell would go up, "That's right, Mark Baby, go tell your daddy about it."

During the heat and excitement of a game, I doubt that Mark ever looked over and said to himself as he passed the puck, "I'm passing it to my father." He was simply moving it to another linemate. Of course, the Howes have always stuck up for each other. If a player picked a fight with any one of them, he was liable to have all three on his hands.

One night against Edmonton, a free-for-all erupted near the end of the game, with players from both clubs pouring off the bench. The Aeros had the win wrapped up, 6-2, but the fight was still undecided. From the stands you could see a gray head bobbing through the mob of forty players, all squared off and flailing away.

From the middle of the pack, Mark's head surfaced. "Over there, Dad," he yelled at Gordie, pointing across the ice. "Some guy's on top of Marty again."

But it wasn't just Gordie looking after the boys. We were all mother hens—even Cathy. From the stands she would shout down to the rink, *"Don't you dare hit my brother."* I can't imagine what it would be like if Mark and Marty ever wound up on opposing teams. Rooting for both, having to watch one check the other.

During the season the Aeros' Paul Popiel did play against his brother, Jan, who was with Winnipeg. One night Jan traded blows with one of Paul's teammates, and Jan got the worst of it. I wondered what Paul must have been thinking at that moment. It was a variation of the old puzzle—the lady or the tiger? Your brother or your team?

Mark probably explained the whole father-son condition best. When a reporter at midseason asked the eternal question, concerning what it was like to play beside his dad, Mark replied, "It feels like playing with any other hockey player, except he's so much better. But the only time he's my dad is when he's hurt."

They knew it was "Dad" out there the day Gordie hooked skates with Andre Hinse in practice, slid five feet, headfirst, into the boards, and knocked himself out. Cold. When he came to, his first words were to Mark, "Don't tell your mother I hit my head. Just call her and tell her something else."

Gordie had suffered a head injury early in his career, in 1950, that nearly cost him his life. He was one of the last holdouts against wearing a helmet, and I nagged him repeatedly about it.

Mark called, and the first thing he said was, "Dad fell and hit his head."

I'm not sure now which of us was more shaken at the time, me or Andre Hinse, who feared he would be remembered as the fellow who ended Gordie Howe's comeback. Gordie went to the hospital, where he spent the night, with a slight concussion. Andre went to a bar, where he sat alone most of the day.

"Poor Andy," said Mark, "he thought it was all over."

Gordie was released the next day in time to play in that night's game against Toronto. But first, he had to face his nagging wife. He knew he was going to get the "I told you so" number, and he did. Both boys wore helmets and always had. It was just part of their equipment. But Gordie had done so only briefly in his career, twice after he had suffered concussions and on the insistence of the team doctors. Before he joined the Aeros, I tried again to persuade him to wear one.

"They're great," he said, as he always did, "for kids."

You simply can't argue with him. For one thing, in that night's game all he did was pick up three points. His teammates were all set to give him a whack on the head before every game. If they could beat me to it.

Meanwhile, what was happening at the box office had all but established Houston as the crown jewel of the two-year-old World Hockey Association. Season-ticket sales had tripled over the Aeros' first season, when they reached the playoffs and were swept out by Winnipeg in four straight. Crowds of over 8,000 had begun to show up in the cramped Sam Houston Coliseum. On the road they had become the league's best draw.

The city had a fever, and it was typified by a group of fans who called themselves Griff's Army, in honor of a local bar at which they assembled before each game—and frequently when no game was scheduled. They boarded a special bus and arrived en masse, marching in with bagpipers, cheerleaders, and funny signs. Their support could best be described as uninhibited—a few times I thought they would get the whole Coliseum arrested, but their fun was contagious.

Then there was the horn section. I am not certain how many horns there were, beyond a vague impression that there were too many. But each of the *musicians* had a different kind, and they blasted them all night long. Lord help the poor soul who accidentally bought a season ticket for a seat in front of them.

The P.A. announcer, a sadist, would say over the loud-speaker, "Let's hear it from the horn section," and the walls would shake for the next ten minutes. One night a guy un-furled a twenty-foot poster that read, HELP! I AM BEING HELD PRISONER IN THE HORN SECTION. We knew what he meant.

The Houston fans were beautiful. They cheered the good plays. They cheered the bad plays. They cheered the ice-sweeping crew. They cheered everything.

It was like being part of a tidal wave. No one ever accused us of missing a chance to promote hockey. One night, as we left a charity dinner, Gordie and I saw a man jump out of the bushes and snatch a purse from a woman's arm. We leaped into our car and took after the thief, who was on foot. With me riding shotgun and shrieking, "There he goes," Gordie gunned the car, jumped a curb, and drove across a field. At that point the purse snatcher threw his plunder back at us and hightailed it for home.

The woman's husband, who was trailing the action on foot, caught up with us. We introduced ourselves. The husband said, "What can I do to repay you?"

Gordie, never at a loss for words, said, "Well, you can buy some tickets and come down and see the Aeros play."

Boy, his admiring teammates said later, that Gordie will do *anything* to sell tickets.

He never turned down an invitation to appear at Rotary or Lion's Club meetings. At one such function, he was introduced by Jim Smith, who said he felt Gordie was owed a public apology for having to play in a coliseum that was forty-five years old, which was Jim's way of hinting that the city needed to get on with plans for a new arena. Gordie chose not to take it quite that way.

"Now wait a minute," he said, "we don't have to apologize for anything that's forty-five years old."

Somehow, in the mysterious way that sports can produce such chemistry, all those strangers of a few weeks before became a team. They were playing superb hockey, and they seemed to have an honest, good-natured affection for each other. They were constantly playing tricks.

Paul Popiel was the team intellectual—meaning that he read books—and on one trip someone carefully tore out the last six pages of his current mystery novel. They were flying along, and all of sudden Paul let out a scream that probably woke the copilot.

"Okay," he wailed, "which one of you bastards did it?"

He spent weeks trying to find another copy of that book so he could learn how the story ended. I'm not sure that he ever did.

By the Christmas holidays we all sensed that the Aeros were going the full course. Gordie was back in the milestone business. He had found a good luck charm, a little girl who sat with her dad in the Booster Club section, next to the place where the players came on and off the ice. Gordie always gave her a gentle pat or rub on the head, and I know she felt personally responsible for whatever goals he might score that night.

The little girl must have been ready for heaven, along with 7,900 other fams, the night Gordie scored four goals in one game for the first time in his career. This was instantly labeled the "Texas hat trick"—*everything* is bigger in Texas. On the receiving end were the Los Angeles Sharks in a game the entire Houston team almost missed, which should have told us right there how the season was going.

They were grounded in Toronto the morning of the game by a snowstorm, had to charter a flight, needed a police escort to get to the Coliseum, and arrived a half-hour late, holding up the face off while they hurriedly dressed. By all the laws of reason, Gordie and his mates should have been dog tired. But he slapped in four goals, just missed two others, and Houston coasted to an 8–3 victory.

Gordie told the press that night that this season was the most fun he had ever had, and I know he meant it. He wasn't being disloyal to the memory of those great years and great teams in Detroit. But this was different. He was in business with his sons. He was young again. There was nothing that could compare to it.

I was wet-eyeball happy myself that night because my fourth hockey player, Murray, was home for the holidays, in the seat next to mine. We accused Gordie of showing off for the youngest member of the family. Murray flew back to Detroit with quite a story to tell.

Murray is that happy combination of brain and brawn. He takes karate and loves to read and passes as the family wit. I telephoned on his last birthday and started singing "Happy Birthday." He listened, then said, "Is this a crank call?" Once, after hearing Gord and me discuss our wills, he asked what would happen to him if we both died. I told him he could live with Bill and Edna Gadsby. He cracked, "With four girls—I'd rather go to an orphanage." Murray has a soft face and wavy hair, and he's the only one with Gordie's eyes—hazel.

Milestones usually add pressure. The great athletes can't wait to get them, like Satan, behind them. There is always so much talk about when The Goal is going to come. For Gordie those special plateaus have always been a curse. I can't recall how many games passed between his 799th and 800th goals, which he scored for the Aeros on January 17, 1974; I only know that we thought it would never come.

Gordie had reached his first magic number on October 27, 1963, when his 544th goal tied the record of Montreal's own Maurice Richard. He scored it, in fact, against the Canadiens, who in a fine and sporting gesture planned to present him with a portrait to commemorate the next one, number 545, the record breaker. The game would be stopped, when and wherever it happened, and the painting presented to Gordie.

Two weeks passed. Some poor fellow had to haul that package all over the northlands, from town to town, while Gordie struggled to get the goal. As fate would have it, he scored this one, too, against Montreal, at the Olympia, with Charley Hodge in the net. But it took so long they nearly had to age the painting. The years rolled by, and in December of 1968 at Pittsburgh, he produced his 700th goal—with a stick borrowed from teammate Bruce MacGregor.

Number 800 had a personal touch. It came against the Vancouver Blazers, off a goalie named Peter Donnelly, a product of the Detroit amateur hockey leagues whose younger brother had been a teammate of Mark and Marty Howe. When writers asked how he felt about giving up Gord's 800th goal, Peter replied, "Proud."

Life would have been perfect, except we were all still waiting for Marty to score his first goal as a pro. His defensive skills were getting stronger with each game. But that goal! It wasn't so much to ask, when his father had so many and his younger brother was among the league leaders. When it finally came, I waited outside the dressing room to congratulate him, a little unsettled that it had arrived at a moment when I was displeased with Marty over a matter of social import.

I felt he had not treated a certain young woman properly. I

wasn't trying to matchmake. I just wanted him to observe the rules. He had invited her to Houston, and she had traveled a long way to visit him. Later, the Aeros appeared in her city for a game, and I am quite sure she expected to hear from him. But Marty had arranged a date with another girl, on the same night the rest of the Howes were meeting the first girl's family after the game. Marty ducked out and left Mark and Gordie to cover for him.

It isn't easy to get mad at Marty. He's the quiet one, blond, good looking, with a sensitive, almost nineteenth-century quality. Mark has a boyish pug face. Marty, with his long hair and mustache, could model for a cameo.

But I had let him know how I felt. His conduct was unsporting, I said.

Marty walked out of the dressing room, spotted me, walked over and held out his hand. "Mom," he said, "I've got something for you." He put the puck in my hand, the one with which he scored his first goal. "Because," he said, "you're the best mother in the whole world."

That's another thing, dammit. Marty could sweet-talk his way out of anything. "Marty," I said, "you'll never go wrong with a line like that." It is a useful quality in a person, to know how to set things right.

The spring of the year went Mark's way—he produced his first hat trick—but not Gord's. He spent his forty-sixth birthday, on March 31, with his foot in a cast. During a game against the New England Whalers, he had caught a blasting shot on his instep in the final minute. He tried to play on it for a week, but the foot kept getting worse. When it was x-rayed a hairline fracture showed up, and with the division title already sewed up, the Aeros decided he should rest it, in the hope it would heal for the playoffs. The cast went on, and Gordie went off the ice for ten days.

The raves were coming now. In March, *Sports Illustrated* was on the stands with Gordie on the cover and a tagline that read: AMAZING GORDIE HOWE—NO. 1 AT 45. A story inside said flatly he had the league's Most Valuable Player award locked up, and he was the father of the likely Rookie of the Year, Mark.

At the time, Gordie led the league in scoring, though his idleness would drop him to third place in the final listing. Nothing and nobody could shed rain on his parade now—not even a little needling from an old friend. *Sports Illustrated* quoted Ted Lindsay, who had teamed with Gordie and Sid Abel on the original production line, as saying the W.H.A. must be a sorry league if a forty-five-year-old relic, coming off two years' retirement, could be the leading scorer.

Gordie answered by pointing out that he was forty-one when he had his most productive year in Detroit, with 103 points. He finished third in the race that season, behind Phil Esposito and Bobby Hull.

With Gordie back in the lineup, the Aeros did win it all, roaring back from two games down to drop Minnesota from the playoffs, then blitzing the Chicago Cougars in four. They had won the AVCO Cup and given Houston, a city starved for a winner, its first pro championship team in something like fifteen years.

Talk about your dream season. Gordie had set a target of seventy points for himself. He had an even one hundred, on thirty-one goals and sixty-nine assists. Mark finished with seventy-nine points, including thirty-eight goals.

For the inside hockey nut the plus figures had more significance. Hockey coaches use a system in which each player on the ice gets a plus when his team scores a goal, a minus when they yield one. The pluses and minuses are given only when the teams are at equal strength. Gordie led the Aeros with a plus fifty-five. Mark was second with a plus fifty-three. Marty scored a thirty-eight, super for a defenseman.

The scene after the championship game was a cross between a Marx Brothers comedy and the running of the bulls at Pamplona. Bagpipes squealed, horns blared, fans embraced, and half-naked players chased each other through the locker room with fizzing bottles of champagne.

In the confusion, Gordie and I ducked out for the victory celebration that had been hastily arranged at the Whitehall Hotel—where we had spent our first night in Houston, eight months before.

I had driven to the game in Marty's car and left it for him at the Coliseum. An hour later Marty arrived at the party. "Did anybody bring Mark?" he asked.

Gordie and I exchanged quick looks. "We thought he was with you." Just as we were starting to grab our coats, Mark walked in the door.

"Thanks a heap. Big rookie star gets left at the rink," he cracked.

It was just one more notation in an endless list of times the Howes had left one of the kids at the rink. We all laughed. It wasn't hard to do when your team has just won a championship, and you have seen a city transformed.

Driving home much later we stopped for coffee in a twenty-four-hour diner, just to unwind, to talk, to prolong the night. I thought about how strange it had all seemed at first—my impatience when people didn't recognize Gordie, the feeling you had of trying to teach someone a foreign language. The Aeros, at the beginning of the season, hadn't even realized they needed a security guard at the locker room door.

After one game Mark heard a knock and opened the door. An attractive young girl was standing there, peeking inside. "I'd like to have the Howes' autographs," she said.

"Gordie Howe?" asked Mark.

She nodded.

"And Marty Howe?"

"Oh yes."

"What about Mark Howe?"

"Oh yes, he's my favorite."

"Just a minute," he said. "I'll see if I can get them." In a moment he came back with all three, never told her who he was, and closed the door behind him, giggling like a schoolboy.

Now Gordie and I were waiting to give our order in a coffee shop on the Katy Freeway, and in the booth behind us we could overhear four men talking about *that* night's game. Gordie grinned when he heard his own name mentioned in almost-godlike terms. Then the waitress walked up, and Gordie ordered two coffees, one with, one without. The conversation in the booth behind us stopped.

"It's him," one of the men hissed. "It's Gordie Howe."

"Naw, it can't be."

"It is, I tell you. It's *him*."

"Naw," said the other. "What would Gordie Howe be doing in a dump like this?"

We smiled and nodded at them on our way out. I wanted to stop and tell them that Gordie Howe and his sons had been in the right place at the right time all year. But Gordie took my arm and guided me through the door and into the car.

As we drove off, I switched on the radio. I wanted to hear something soft, something by Sinatra, maybe the one about fairy tales coming true. I was in that kind of mood. But the only station I could bring in clearly was playing a record by a group that sounded like a team in the World Football League, whose music drowned out the words, which I wouldn't have understood anyway.

I thought to myself, Mark and Marty would like that. I turned off the radio, and put my head on Gordie's shoulder.

4
From the Potato Patch

IN GORDIE'S LATER SEASONS with Detroit, I kept a candy bar or an orange in my purse to give him after a game so he could pick up some quick energy. I had seen him so weak and drained he would get the shakes while signing autographs. But he always signed for anyone who asked.

He was splendid at it. Not all athletes are. He made the kids say the magic words, "please" and "thank you." He kibitzed and joked and teased with them. He would scribble his name and, without looking up, flick the pen and leave a dot on the boy's nose. The crowd would love it, and some kid from Chicago or Bloomfield wouldn't wash his nose for a week.

Years ago, after a playoff game in Toronto, I waited in the wind and chill outside the Maple Leaf Gardens while Gordie worked his way to the curb, signing programs and notepads and scraps of paper. Standing to one side, I usually had a good vantage point to observe these scenes. And I always ended up going home with a broken heart for the ones who didn't get their autographs. There was even a limit to how long Gordie Howe could stay in one spot signing his name.

This night my wandering eye singled out a small, ordinary-looking boy who could not have been more than ten years old. He had brown hair, big, intense eyes, and he wore the uniform of all young Canadian males—a battered hockey jacket. He seemed alone. There were no adults holding his hand or pushing him to the front of the pack.

Every time he got within ten feet of Gordie, the movement of the older boys shoved him back. It was like watching the tide come in and out. For every step he edged forward, someone knocked him back two. Talk about elbows, this crowd had them. I wish I had had a whistle.

He tried to go under, around, inside, using every trick in the book, but he couldn't get through. The kids sensed that Gordie wouldn't stay much longer. I started hoping he would spot the boy. Finally, Gordie looked my way and gave a headshake, meaning "It's time to scram. Get a cab." I felt sorry for the boy. But Gordie had been signing for thirty minutes and I knew he had to be ready to crash.

I hailed a cab, opened the door, motioned to Gordie, and slid inside. He was right behind me. So was the crowd. As he started to duck into the cab, the kids surged after him as if Gord were the Pied Piper. I looked back and saw the ten-year old leading the chase. He waved his tattered paper and pen in the air and he had the panic-stricken look of a stock broker about to miss the 7:05 commuter train.

The kid stopped in his tracks, half-shouted and half-panted, "Wait for *me*, Gordie. *I've been waiting for you all my life.*"

Never have I seen anyone straighten up and do a U-turn like I saw Gordie do that night. There was no way he could have gotten into that cab and closed the door in the boy's face—no one could. As long as I live, I won't forget the words, the tone of that little would-be hockey player.

It was, I thought, such a lovely and haunting sentence. Don't we all have someone we waited for *all our lives*? For that boy, at that particular instant in his life, it was Gordie Howe. For others, it may have been a John Kennedy or an Arnold Palmer or maybe someone whose name no one else had ever heard. Maybe that's what games are all about. I think we need heroes. There will always be argument over that, whether it is healthy to bathe in someone else's glory. But I think we need them—kids especially. The world still wants to be on the side of the good guys.

I suppose the little boy saw Gordie as a tough character, someone with guts. But there is also a felt pride, a decency, that comes across to kids. It really chills me to see a hero type behave rudely to a fan.

Gordie and the entire Howe clan try to live up to the good guy image—we believe in it and practice it. The way Gordie U-turned for that hockey tyke told me a lot, it reaffirmed what I knew about my husband. He has respect and feeling for his fans, for people.

It was a small moment, but I learned from it. I realized this was the ultimate goal, the ultimate playoff, the ultimate record. To be someone that other people would "wait for all their lives." There could be no higher compliment.

And, I guess, if there ever was anyone I waited for, it was Gord.

We met, not—as you might think — at an ice rink, as did so many hockey couples, but at a bowling alley called The Lucky Strike. It was just down the street from the Olympia. I was seventeen, working as a secretary for a few months before going to college. My stepdad, Budd Joffa, and I met once a week. After the league play finished, we'd stay and bowl a few extra frames together for Cokes.

Gordie had just finished his fifth season with the Red Wings, had led the league in scoring, and was hanging around Detroit for a few weeks, waiting to go on a vacation trip to Florida with some of his teammates. He wandered into the bowling alley fairly often and, I learned later, had been checking me out.

Finally he asked Joe Evans, the alley manager, to introduce us one night. Dad was visibly impressed, but I knew nothing about hockey, and the name Gordie Howe didn't mean a thing. Later, I did vaguely recall hearing Dad talk about some terrible injury this Gordie Howe person had suffered during the Stanley Cup, whatever that was. But at the time the meter didn't register.

He asked if he could drive me home, but I told him, no thanks, I had my car. I thought he was cute, and I adored his suede sportcoat, the most expensive I had ever seen. But I was going steady with a baseball player I had dated all through school.

Gordie didn't give up. He got my number from Joe, through Dad, and called me. We talked for up to three hours at a time, several nights running, but we'd always hang up without Gordie having asked me for a date. I couldn't decide if he was shy, slow, or had a system.

After a week, he asked if I'd like to see a movie. By this time I was curious, intrigued with this guy whose voice I knew much better than his face. The ball player was away for the summer. I said, yes.

Whatever show we saw that night, it made no lasting impression. But Gordie did. I was seventeen, the age every woman wishes she could be at least twice, and I kept wondering if Gordie was going to put his arm around me or not. Thinking back, it was much like a scene out of *Summer of '42*.

Afterward, we dropped into Carl's Chop House on Grand River, just down the block from the Olympia. Over the shrimp cocktail, on this our very first date, Gordie looked up and asked me, "How old do you think a fella should be before he gets married?"

I was so startled I didn't know what to answer. I thought,

how odd—is this guy trying to score points, or is he that naive? The subject didn't come up again for a long, long time.

We went out every night until Gordie left with his friends for Florida. He introduced me to his roommate, Ted Lindsay, which was like introducing me to family. Ted was dating a girl named Pat, who also ended up marrying her hockey player. I knew I was in love. I broke off with the baseball guy. That summer, when Gordie went back to Canada, we both still dated others but we wrote almost daily—long, loving, silly letters.

When Gordie returned and the season started, I got my first taste of what it would be like to marry a pro athlete. At that time, the club made frequent, often last-minute demands on the players. Often the guy would have to cancel a date to appear at a banquet or something. Banquets? I didn't know from banquets. They didn't sound very important to me.

Gord had just gotten off the first road trip, and Friday night's game was going to be our big night. I could think about staying out late and not having to get up and go to work the next morning. That afternoon, he called. He had been drafted for a banquet after the game. I was shattered.

While I was feeling sorry for myself, an old beau called, and I thought, "Well, Mr. Howe, you can have your banquets. I'm not going to sit home."

We went to a concert by The Four Freshmen, a popular group of that day, later part of the nostalgia boom that swept the seventies. Near the end of the show, Gordie walked in with several of the fellows from the banquet. I almost passed out. They joined a girl one of the players was dating and, as bad luck would have it, she was sitting in the booth next to mine.

Gordie couldn't miss me. He gave me a long, pained look and turned away. I thought, *this is the end*. Armageddon.

On game days, Gord had always called and said, "There's a ticket for you at the gate. See you afterwards." The next day I waited for the call that never came. I sat there and died the death of a thousand cuts. He was *never* going to call again. So I took matters into my own hands and did what was, for the early fifties, a very brazen thing. I called *him*.

"Well, hello," I cooed. "I just wanted to tell you I got a ticket for the game (I covered by buying my own), and I'm coming down tonight."

"That's nice." He was so cool my ears were numb.

I said, "Maybe we could see each other after the game."

Mr. Cool said, "That would be fine, except I have a date."

I hung up, crushed but not defeated. I went to the game that night and proceeded to pull a trick that stayed on my conscience for years. I knew quite well where his date would be sitting. After all, it was *my* seat, next to his landlady, Ma Shaw. I marched down the aisle and leaned down beside Ma Shaw. In a nice, clear voice I said, "Ma, would you mind giving Gord a message for me? Tell him I'm sorry I had to break our date tonight, but I'll speak with him tomorrow."

I smiled sweetly and walked back to my seat. Poor Ma Shaw; I put her in a terrible position. I'm sure she never said a word to Gordie. And he never really understood why his date was in such a sour mood. It was years after we were married before I ever told him this story.

When we made up, as I knew we would, he forgave me for not knowing about banquets, and I forgave him for not knowing about women.

We were married in the spring of 1953, without a formal engagement. I pointed out to Gordie we had been courting for three years. I didn't believe in engagements or sitting home all summer staring at a ring on my third finger, left hand. I held out for marriage. What was more, I flatly refused to go to Canada with him to meet his family unless I was his wife. I worried that his parents would disapprove, that no girl could be good enough for their son. I needed some security—say, a marriage license—before I met his family.

Of course, we did meet and I came to have great affection

and respect for them. Gord's parents were your classic, salt-of-the-earth folk. You only had to look at the calluses on their hands to read their lives. I had grown up modestly in Detroit, not remembering my father, but my childhood was a lark compared to Gordie's.

Nine days after he was born on a farm in Floral, Canada, his family moved to Saskatoon. Those were depression years, bleak ones for homesteaders. Gordie was the fifth of nine children. His mother, Katherine, whom he once described as "the strongest woman I ever knew," gave birth to most of them alone, while Ab Howe was out in the fields. The family diet consisted largely of oatmeal, often three times a day. Once, Gordie's dad, out of shotgun shells, ran down a coyote with his bare hands, slit its hind legs, and sold the pelt to buy grain and flour.

Gordie was six when he received his first pair of skates through an act of providence. A lady came to the door selling a bag of used clothes for fifty cents. His mother traded milk stamps for it, and immediately Gordie began to dive into the sack. Buried at the bottom was a pair of skates, much too big for him. But he layered his feet with four or five pairs of heavy woolen socks, and tried them out right away.

From that moment on, hockey was never far from his thoughts. From dawn until dusk and sometimes after dark he skated on the slews—the frozen potato patches of Canada. A neighbor lady kept a supply of tennis balls in her oven for him. When she wasn't home, he'd be out there anyway, in weather forty and fifty degrees below, using "road apples"—frozen horse chips—for pucks. He saved syrup labels to collect hockey cards.

It was not hard to look at Gordie, to talk with him, and see the bones of the boy who used to be showing through. He was painfully shy and overgrown for his age and the kids at school teased him and called him *doughhead*. His mother once told a writer about the day Gordie, a gentle, clumsy lad of nine or ten, came home after failing for a second time to pass the third grade.

"He wasn't bad at school. He always tried. But the second time he failed it took the heart right out of him. I remember seeing him come down the street crying. I said, 'Sit down, Gordie, tell me what's wrong. Is the work too difficult? Don't you understand the teacher? Do you *ask* her questions about what you don't understand?'

"He said, 'No, Mum, I don't want to bother her.' And then we both had a good cry."

He struggled through the eighth grade. Whether he knew it then or not, hockey was his only ticket out of the poverty and potato patches of Saskatoon.

Gordie would sit for hours with his mother in the kitchen while she peeled apples and did her chores.

"You know, Mum," he would say, "when I grow up I'll make something of myself. I'm going to have money and I'm going to buy you things—a stove and a refrigerator. And I'm going to put a toilet in your house. Then, when I'm rich, I'm going to buy you a new house."

He was sensitive even as a child. He felt badly about how hard his mother had to work. Ab Howe tried valiantly to provide for his family, but the times were stacked against him.

Poor as they were, however, their life was not without charm. Dad Howe played the fiddle and they often went to local barn dances. Everyone encouraged Gordie's talent for hockey. He played for fun and for marshmallows—those were the stakes, a welcome change from oatmeal.

His early background never embarrassed him, with one exception. He didn't want anyone to know his family didn't have an indoor toilet. When Gordie turned pro, that was one of the first things he corrected. In a few years, he kept his promise to buy his parents a new home.

He was like a lot of men who were shaped by that era, who saw poverty not as something to be ashamed of but as a condition to be conquered. Early hardship made him humble, and later, big money made him grateful. To this day he doesn't mind washing the windows of his own home or doing what other men might think of as menial jobs. Gordie worked all his life to give his children more than he had had as a youngster, but I suspect he became a better man because of the things he didn't have.

At fifteen he was invited by the New York Rangers to a training camp in Winnipeg. It was the first time he had ever left Saskatoon. He didn't own a white shirt or a tie, and I doubt that he had more than one pair of shoes. He didn't know what real hockey gear was, having used newspapers for shin pads. When equipment was issued to him, he didn't know how to put it on so he dropped it on the floor and watched the other fellows. Most of them laughed at him. After a few days Gordie, who had made no real impression on the Rangers, quit the camp. He hitchhiked back to Saskatoon, hurt and disappointed and homesick for a more familiar life.

The next year a scout for the Red Wings named Fred Pinckney spotted Gordie playing in amateur league. He bought him a suit and a pair of shoes and coaxed him into going to the Red Wings' camp at Windsor, Ontario. There he caught the eye of Jack Adams, who never tired of telling the story of the first time he saw Gordie Howe.

He always told it the same way: "I noticed him go in on the net and fire a shot with one hand, then come back and fire a shot with the other. So I called out, 'Hey, son, let's see you do that again.' He did. Then I called him over to the boards and said, 'What's your name, son?' A lot of kids that age would choke up when they start talking to you. But this one just looked me in the eye and said, real easy-like, 'My name is Howe, but I'm no relation to that one over there.'

"He was pointing to Syd Howe, one of our leading scorers. I said, 'If you practice hard enough and try hard enough maybe you'll be as good someday.'"

Jack signed him to his first contract and sent him to the farm team at Galt, Ontario, where he worked out with the team and played only in exhibition contests. There was a problem clearing his transfer papers from Western Canada.

The next season he was assigned to the Red Wings' farm at Omaha. He scored twenty-two goals, turned eighteen and proved himself a fighter. One day he jumped off the bench and decked an opponent who had bullied an Omaha teammate.

"What's the matter?" his coach, Tommy Ivan, kidded him. "Don't you like that fellow?"

Gordie growled back, "I don't like any of them."

That remark traveled straight to Detroit, where Jack Adams decided he was ready. The next year Gordie made the big team, although his first ten games with the Red Wings were distinguished only by the fact that he got into ten straight fights.

"Okay, son," Jack told him. "You've convinced me you can fight. Now let's see if you can play hockey."

He scored his first goal, the first of all those hundreds, on October 16, 1946, against Toronto and a goalie named Turk Broda. He scored only six more the rest of the season, most of which he spent in the penalty box or on the bench. He was just learning to play cribbage, and he passed the time by figuring out cribbage plays in his head.

"If Adams had known," he said, "he probably would have killed me."

It wasn't until his second season that Gordie tugged the now famous Number Nine jersey over his head. He claimed it, very simply, for reasons that had to do with train travel. In those days lower berths were assigned to players with low numbers, since those generally belonged to the veterans. But Roy Connacher, who wore Nine before Gordie, had been traded that summer of 1947. Having slept in an upper as a rookie (seventeen), he wasted no time in grabbing it.

In November of that year, the Red Wings established Sid Abel, Ted Lindsay, and Gordie as a regular line. They were to become one of the famous combinations of sport—The Production Line. They were a machine, three men playing as one. They had a kind of extrasensory perception on the ice, an instinct for knowing where the others were, almost what they were *thinking*. Often you can take three of the most talented hockey players and put them together and nothing happens. But in this case the chemistry worked. They had an instinctive sense for making the right move at the right time that was deadly.

Teamwork in hockey demands more resourcefulness than most sports. Unlike football, the plays are not fully orchestrated. The key is in anticipating what another player will do, and The Production Line did it uncannily. When the line broke up in 1952, Detroit tried out player after player to fill Sid Abel's center spot. But never again was there a line with the same magic.

Much of this, of course, I learned later, as my interest in hockey warmed. I knew nothing of Gordie's career, firsthand, before 1950, and by the time I was sitting regularly in his seat at the Olympia he was already well established and a member of the All-Star team each year.

In that 1950 season he suffered the injury that almost ended his career and his life, during the week of his twenty-second birthday. Some years later I went back and looked up the newspaper clippings. He had collided with Ted Kennedy, captain of the Maple Leafs, and crashed headfirst into the boards. He suffered a brain concussion, among lesser injuries such as a broken cheekbone and nose, and a lacerated eyeball. When pressure began to build at the base of his skull, surgery had to be performed to relieve it. His mother and sister rushed to his side, and he was on the critical list for days.

The injury left his optic nerve slightly haywire, and he

suffered with double vision for the rest of that summer. In the years since then he has broken ribs, wrists, toes, and shoulders. I'm thankful that I got to miss at least one mishap.

What I learned about hockey in those years came less from Gordie than from Jack Adams. He was the one constant factor in Detroit, the one link to the past, to the beginning. He was tough, harsh, iron-fisted, and we loved him. He gave us both a sense of discipline. He never let you know how he felt, but let someone else say something unkind and he was the first to come to your defense. He never failed to praise Gordie in his speeches or in his interviews as the best hockey player he ever saw. But he never said it to his face.

He was famous for telling the players, after a losing effort, "You should have paid your own way into the game."

When things went badly he spared no one. One night, Gordie scored a hat trick, but the Red Wings lost, 4–3. In the dressing room, Jack tongue-lashed them all, then he turned to Gordie. "And you," he said with contempt. "Three goals, wasted. Why didn't you save them for some night when we could use them?"

If a player angered Jack Adams, he was banished instantly to a farm team in the outback, there to make his move or be lost in the shuffle. I doubt if Jack could last in hockey today, or in pro sports, for that matter. His style was effective because only six teams existed, and there were players standing in line to take your place. In later years, a coach who applied his own form of discipline risked cries of oppression, and players would run to their lawyers, demanding their civil rights.

Times do change, often for the better. The standard of living for hockey players in those days was slightly above that of migrant fruit pickers. The average salary was around $5,000 a year, and through most of the fifties Gordie needed a summer job to make ends meet. By the second half of the decade, with a few endorsements and bonuses, he reached the $20,000 bracket. He was one of the best-known and best-paid players in hockey.

We lived comfortably in those years. By the standards of the sport we were considered well-to-do because we owned two cars. Hockey people car–pooled long before it was patriotic, and it had nothing to do with the ecology. Many of the players of that era were rough, uneducated, had little money to spend, and no real future for which to save.

It was a passionate sport, played in old arenas, usually in rough neighborhoods, before emotional crowds. Part of the excitement came from finding out what was left of your car when the game ended, and you returned to the parking lot. At the Olympia, street kids would charge a dollar to "protect" your car. You usually paid, if you wanted your hubcaps and windshield to be there when you got back.

Once, Gordie left his car at the stadium for a short road trip, along with mine, which had been loaned to a player new to the team. When the Red Wings got back to town, *both* cars were missing.

The years just fled by, with each new milestone going up like a flare in Gordie's career. In 1963, against Montreal, appropriately, he tied and broke the lifetime scoring record of Maurice Richard—544 goals. So many seasons, so many nice moments, frozen in time like a butterfly sealed in amber.

There was Gordie Howe Night, in 1959, at the Olympia, when a brand new car, wrapped in cellophane, was driven onto the ice for Gord. The big surprise was inside: his mother and dad, who had never seen their son compete in the National Hockey League. When they stepped out of the car, Gordie put his head on his mother's shoulder and wept like a baby.

For the longest time it seemed as if nothing but success could come our way. Gordie's 600th goal was made a bit more memorable by the reaction of one of his young teammates. To celebrate the goal, the management held a special promotion in which pucks were to be given to the first 600 fans through the turnstile. A rookie, Bryan Watson, stood in line before the game, with the fans, and picked up his souvenir puck. He came running into the dressing room, elated, waving it proudly. The other Red Wings couldn't believe it. They practically fell on the floor laughing. But Bryan's act of devotion touched Gord. He was a sweet, refreshing kid and we both had affection for him.

But Gordie's most impressive record was simply his longevity. We were reminded of that in 1971 when we were invited to the American Airlines celebrity golf event in which pro athletes of all sports mingle. As Gord and I danced after the lovely dinner, I thought how lucky we had been to hang on long enough to see the changes. Hockey had expanded across the continent, salaries had boomed, and the exposure was reaching new millions of people. Best of all, hockey players were no longer considered jocks or treated as cattle on skates. They were welcomed to the family of professionals.

That night, when we returned to our room, there was a message to telephone our cottage at Bear Lake. Gord's parents were staying there with the children. A friend, Randy Omer, answered our call and said, "Let me talk to you first, Colleen. Then I think you'll want to put Gordie on. His mother has had a fall. They've taken her away in an ambulance. We think she is dead."

My hand went limp and the phone dropped from my hand. Gordie picked it up. Then he didn't say a word. He just broke down. It had been only a few weeks before that his mother had kissed Gord, at the end of a visit, and then fought back tears. I had asked her what was wrong. "I've never seen you like this."

She said, "As you get older, you are always afraid that each time you say good-by will be the last you'll see of your children."

Gordie was never too proud, too much a man, to shed honest tears. In some families the love is never really allowed to show. It wasn't like that with the Howes. What they felt, what they shared, how they expressed it, was always of some meaning to me. I had grown up with a lot of divorce around me, raised by an aunt and uncle until my mother remarried.

Her second husband, Budd Joffa, adopted me and was the only dad I knew through the first half of my life. I had never met my real father, and had not expected to, until one day, quite literally out of the blue, he called. By then I had a family of my own, already half-grown. He wanted to see me, talk with me. Why all those years later? I didn't know. Conscience? Curiosity? I never found out.

We did meet, however, and I discovered a nice stranger from whom I had inherited some of my looks and some of my disposition. He had started a new life after he and my mother divorced, had fathered another family and invited me, and mine, to visit them on Thanksgiving Day. They had lived in Detroit all that time. I grew up an only child, and I would have enjoyed meeting my half-brothers and sisters.

But a few minutes before we were to leave the house, he called and asked us not to come. When they learned I existed, his other family had not accepted it well. He thought it best that we postpone the visit.

I don't believe I suffered from what drugstore psychologists today like to call an identity crisis. I have enjoyed being who and what I am. Although there were certainly moments during Gordie's twenty-five years on ice when his fans overran me. Once, a woman just barged into our home and took Gordie to task for allowing his photo to be used in a liquor ad.

When he suffered with his arthritis problems, fans from all over the map wrote in, offering their cures and home remedies. One fellow told him to place two or three small potatoes in his pocket and continue to play until the potatoes putrefied. I picked that letter out of his fan mail and showed it to Gord. He read it, looked up, and said, "Idaho or Irish?"

It was heady stuff to walk into a fine restaurant, be recognized by the maitre d', and escorted to the best table in the house; or to meet someone whose talent you had admired, such as the actress Mitzi Gaynor and learn that she was a Gordie Howe fan.

Then there was the summer he made a trip to his old hometown, Saskatoon, after one of his finest Red Wing seasons. An old timer stopped him on the street, said hello, and gave him a quizzical look. "I never see you around here in the winter," the old fellow said. "Where the hell do you go?"

Anytime he starts to take the fame game seriously, or I do, we remind each other of that summer in Saskatoon.

Of course, in any business that depends on the interest and emotion of the public, you don't expect to win them all. You just want to hold down the score. Long ago I lost track of the wacky calls Gordie has received. One day a lady called who insisted she was his "biggest fan." She was adamant about it. And she really meant it. It developed that she weighed 250 pounds, really was his biggest fan, and wanted Gordie's help in persuading the Olympia to widen its seats.

Inevitably, the fans confuse the players' wives. There was one elderly lady, who was lame and attended the games alone for years. One night, before a playoff contest, I was sipping a cup of coffee in the hallway when she walked past me. I said hello. Having seen her so many times I felt as though we knew each other. We chatted about the series and then, somehow, the subject turned to hockey wives. She said, "The one I can't stand is Mrs. Howe."

I almost spilled my coffee. "Do you know my name?" I asked, smiling.

"Aren't you Mrs. Kelly?"

"No. I'm Mrs. Howe."

The poor woman turned pale. I helped her to her seat and told her not to worry, I was just pleased that we had cleared up the mistaken identity. I never did figure out which wife she thought was Mrs. Howe. That was the last time I ever saw her at a Red Wings' game, and I have felt guilty about it all these years.

The last seasons of discontent in Detroit, even the slights when we left, were only flyspecks compared to all the great years, the joy, the oddball things. Jack Adams once said, "Hockey to Gordie is fun, and he will be great as long as it remains that way. Personally, I can't foresee the day when the game *won't* be fun for him."

The day did come, of course—September 7, 1971. Gordie announced his retirement after twenty-five years, 1,841 games, and 853 goals. In March of 1972 they retired his jersey at the Olympia. A crowd of more than 14,000 turned out, including the governor and the mayor. President Nixon sent a personal message and the then vice-president, Spiro Agnew, was on hand to read it; there was a little quip about the fans of America wishing they could keep Gordie "on ice."

When it was his turn, Gordie began, "Everyone is here but one person . . ."—meaning his mother—and then for a few moments the words wouldn't come out. I doubt there were many dry eyes in the stadium. It is a rare day, when you feel so close to people, and your friends are all around you, and you can hear echoes of the past.

How far Gordie had traveled from that potato patch in Saskatoon to be honored by the heads of state. The only thing was, we had no way of knowing then that it would be merely his Retirement, Part I. As with the movie *The Godfather*, there would have to be a sequel.

5
Cold Hands and Warm Hearts

IT BEGAN, I THINK, the winter Gordie turned thirty-two. Marty was six, Mark was five, and I was exhausted. The other two, Cathy and Murray, were still babies.

We decided to build an ice rink so the kids could skate in their own front yard. This was just one of the cute, traditional things you did when your husband played in the National Hockey League and *his* children needed a convenient place to skate.

The Howes weren't the only nut cases. You would see families all over Canada and the northern United States doing much the same, in the way that fathers in the Midwest and Northeast nail basketball hoops to the garage.

But, trust me about this: with a hoop it's easier.

There was a shortage of ice in Detroit, at least the kind kids could skate on, so until we built the rink Gordie had to improvise. Once, in ten-degree weather, he dropped the boys off at a golf course, part of which had frozen over. During the day it rained, leaving a glaze of ice on the fairways. When Gord returned to pick them up, they had skated the entire eighteen holes. I wondered, at the time, if that was a record.

Now, anyone who saw you constructing an ice rink would instantly conclude that you had been hit by a low-flying puck. But we did it nearly every winter. One year, we won a Civic Club prize when we placed a Christmas tree in each corner of the rink and draped it with lights. The sponsors thought we did it just for the contest. We did it so the kids could skate at night.

The problem is that you can't simply fill an ice rink as you would a swimming pool. Flooding a rink makes bumpy ice. And no hockey player worthy of the name would hear of his kids skating on bumpy ice. So we waited until it was freezing cold, nailed a bunch of two-by-fours together, and covered them with plastic. Then we sprinkled, day and night, around the clock, for about a week. We would each take a shift, lugging the hose in and out of the house each time. When the water made a glaze it was ready for another layer. Members of the sprinkling crew set their alarm clocks for each shift.

During one of my wee-hour turns, I came to the stark realization that I had lost my mind. There I stood at four A.M., in a freezing wind, in my flannel nightgown, Gordie's ski parka, boots, and gloves—spraying water all over my crabgrass. I was still there one morning when the milkman pulled into the driveway. I will give him credit. It was one of the bravest attempts to appear nonchalant in the presence of a crazy woman I have ever seen. He touched the bill of his cap, said, "Good morning, Mrs. Howe," and toted his milk basket up the steps as though all the housewives on his route were outside at dawn, in the dead of winter, watering their lawns.

I rolled my eyes and thought, "Boy, what I won't sacrifice so my kids can play hockey."

In the summer the boys put on their bathing suits and played hockey in the driveway, on the concrete. Year round, our house looked like a training room. We were up to our knees in hockey gear. I would have to wade through it just to reach the kitchen.

Those were sweet years for any parent, when each day brought some new awareness to your children. Marty was furious with all of us when he came home from his very first day at school.

"Why didn't you tell me?" he demanded.

"Tell you what?"

"Why didn't you tell me my dad is a hockey star?"

Around our home, what Gordie did for a living had simply never been an issue. I doubt that it is in many homes, when kids are still in the toy gun and doll stage. They didn't read the papers, and their taste in television fare ran to cartoons. All they knew was that Daddy spent a lot of nights at the rink.

Once, Mark answered the phone and the caller inquired if his father was at work. "No," said Mark. "My dad doesn't work. He plays hockey."

Marty was astounded when he enrolled in grade school and found that the other children knew who Gordie Howe was and where Marty lived. He acted as though I had been withholding information from him. But it didn't take him long to realize he was on to a good thing. Soon I noticed he was coming home with a model car, some jacks, or a paddle ball. I decided I had best find out the source of all this new property.

Matter-of-factly, Marty told me the kids at school had been asking for autographed photos of his dad. He had seized the moment to go into business for himself and was trading the pictures for merchandise. As much as we favor the free enterprise system, I had to tell the photo hustler his trading post was shut down. If his friends wanted his dad's picture, he was to make them available, compliments of the Howes.

Our boys, and Cathy, too, had skates almost before they cut teeth. Gordie would skate around the Olympia before practice, with one of his offspring perched on his shoulder. And he would teach them to hold onto the back of a chair, while he got in front and pushed it and them around the ice. That's how they learned to skate—through the old chair technique. Gordie laced up their skates, then moved the chair around the rink, letting them use it for balance until they had their skating legs. It wasn't long before they asked for hockey sticks.

Mark was four and Marty five when they joined their first minor league team—the Teamsters' 299. When we said those kids were organized we weren't kidding. It was Jimmy Hoffa's local that sponsored them.

I don't suppose you could describe Mark as a late bloomer. He had his own bona fide hockey bag filled with regulation equipment by the time he got to kindergarten. He couldn't wait to take the gear to school for "show and tell." He told his teacher he wanted to show it to the other kids, because otherwise they wouldn't know what the players wore under their uniforms. I guess Mark didn't want his classmates growing up without knowing that hockey players wore suspenders.

Mark pulled out the shoulder pads and the shin pads and the suspenders, explaining each item. Then he closed his little presentation by reaching into the bottom of the bag and bringing out his cup. "This," he announced, "is my weenie protector."

The teacher and the other students roared. But Mark, when he told us the story later, was furious. This was a piece of equipment from a grown-up man's world. It meant the difference—to him—between being a genuine hockey player and just another kid playing let's pretend.

Many times I have regretted not saving the boys' first skates. But in those years we gave the equipment away as they outgrew it. When boys are little, skates don't get much abuse—they aren't wearing the blades down to nothing—and it seemed a pity not to let some other little boys enjoy them. It wasn't very long before one pair wouldn't get them through a season.

Minor hockey was no cheap trip, although it was less expensive than something like skiing or raising thoroughbreds. The skates we bought the boys cost twenty-nine dollars then, and sell for fifty dollars today. Their gloves were nineteen dollars—around thirty dollars on today's market. I wondered how some parents managed, especially those who had two, three, and four sons in the sport. Besides the equipment there were frequent road trips. Even if you weren't driving, you were putting pocket money in your kid's pants. I know many parents who moonlighted and sacrificed to keep their boys in hockey programs.

Of course, ours grew up with hockey, surrounded by it, but we made a point of exposing them to other things—bowling, camping, skiing. They loved going with Gordie on fishing trips. But the hockey was always there. It was our lighthouse. The Olympia was like a second home.

While the Red Wings dressed after a game, their sons would assemble at the back end of the arena and play minihockey. One night, we forgot to check the kids' action and accidentally left Murray behind after a game. When we discovered we were minus one and rushed back to get him, we found him in the stands, quietly reading a book. I was afraid he would be in distress, but he had calmly told the maintenance man, Quint, "Oh, they'll come back." I knew then that the kids felt as comfortable in the stadium as at home.

There was one time when Gordie nearly exiled Marty—I mean banished him from the Olympia. The kids had joined their father in the dressing room after a loss. There was dead silence; no one spoke as the players watched Jack Adams pace back and forth. Marty finally looked at him and blurted, "Who are you?"

Gordie said as soon as he saw Marty's jaw work he started to clamp his hand over the boy's mouth. But for once his reactions were slow. Adams, the coach who always seemed like such a grump even though he was soft inside, removed the cigar from his lips and said, "My name is Jack Adams. You ask your daddy who I am."

If any of our sons could be called a reluctant hockey player, it would be Marty. When I run across old photographs of Gordie in his first years with Detroit, there is no question: What I see is the face of our younger son, Mark. He is the one I can imagine on the potato patch. Mark was always beside me at Gordie's games, cheering, loving every minute. Marty never cared much for crowds. He has since learned to handle them, but in those earlier days he preferred to stay at home.

A creek ran behind our house in Detroit. Whenever I was looking for Marty that was where I would find him, trying to catch killifish with a net or hook and line or watching turtles. He was at peace fishing, being alone, or enjoying solitude with a friend. It was his way, I think, of losing the crowd and the hubub that went on around our home. The phone was always ringing or someone was waiting for an interview or Gordie was getting ready for a game.

Marty was an end on his high school football team until his coach dismissed him for missing practice one day to play in a key hockey game. I blew my cork. Gordie told Marty to tell his football coach to shove it. But Marty enjoyed football, had wondered if he might be good enough to play in college, and felt badly about giving it up.

Mark, on the other hand, never thought about anything else but hockey. As long as I can remember, he was banging a puck against the garage door, or out in the neighborhood trying to recruit some little kid to play goalie. He thought about being a goalie for a time, but there was just no way, with his speed and moves, a coach was going to leave him in the net.

On nights when Gordie was due home from a road trip, Mark would wait up or set his alarm for one or two A.M. He loved being awake when Gordie walked in, often with two or three of his teammates. On those nights, he would talk me into fixing a pizza and salad for supper. Then he'd say, "We should leave enough in the oven for Dad." When Gordie and his guests walked through the door, Mark had the beers opened for them.

This was his vision of the big leagues. They let him pour half a beer for himself, and Mark thought that was—well— neat. We operated on the theory that what the kids were allowed to do within limits at home, they wouldn't do to excess while hiding around the corner. If we had wine for the holidays or a special occasion, we let them try a glass. We've trusted them, and the system seemed to work, though we kept our fingers crossed.

While our boys were growing up in Detroit, so was amateur hockey. It simply exploded. I was pleased that Gordie and I had been involved in it. Our last year there, at least 300 new teams were organized across the state. Of course, minor hockey in Canada was always a kind of national religion. Over 10,000 fans once turned out in Quebec for a Pee Wee tournament in which Mark and Marty played. The crowd started to find seats at nine in the morning. The boys' game wasn't until nine that night.

As the interest in minor hockey grew in Detroit, sponsors began to appear who were willing to pick up the tab for expenses—up to $10,000 a year. They sometimes bought the complete uniform, easily the most expensive in all sport.

I suppose it is like this wherever kids are absorbed in some activity—hockey or baseball or ballet—your life seems to orbit around them. You develop a separate circle of friends, all part of the same satellite. We called ours the The Rink Rats of America. In Canada, "rink rats" are technically the kids who hang around the rinks, hoping to carry someone's skates or to shovel snow, all just waiting for a chance to make a team. Our kids practically lived at the rink. They seemed part of the woodwork.

We parents adopted that name, The Rink Rats, because it fit. Indoors or out, we hung around the rink, waiting on frozen benches in the splintery bleachers, with red noses and numbed toes, while our kids played hockey. We were the men and women of Sparta, playing our own games of freeze-out. My own record freeze-out—the point at which you gave up and went begging for a fireplace or a Saint Bernard—was fifteen-below at a Pee Wee game in Quebec City. Gordie, who in his boyhood played in minus thirty- and forty-degree weather, always said that was why he never became a goalie. Goalies often froze in their own tracks.

In Gordie's Canada, almost every town, no matter how small, had an indoor ice rink. They usually had a filling station, a grocery, a hardware store and an indoor rink—not necessarily in that order.

With a husband setting records in the National Hockey League and soon three sons playing at various minor levels, I became accepted as the queen of The Rink Rats. Some winters I sat through more than 200 games. One season I logged 10,000 miles on my car, driving from rink to rink all over the northern United States and Canada.

My life revolved around snow tires, four A.M. ice times, and across-the-border car-pooling. This was it—the care and feeding of little hockey people. Gordie was often tied up with his own games, leaving it to Mom to get everyone safely through that night's storm and on to the tournament.

Sometimes we would arrive in a town in weather meant for the beach. When we came out an ice storm might be raging. I'd drive all the way home with two tires on the road and two off, unable to hold the car on the pavement. If the ice storms didn't make you a wreck, the fog off Port Huron did.

One winter Gordie bought me a mink stole. We half-joked about converting it into some nice warm mukluks (Eskimo boots) that I could wear at the rink. That beautiful mink stole hung in the closet like a trophy because we didn't dine out or do lavish social things. Our life was wrapped up in hockey—pro and minor.

For the Howe family those may have been the most contented times of all. We found a wonderful pleasure in each other that made each trip a kind of holiday. All the championship playoffs and White House dinners still to come could not compete with that feeling. Gordie seldom trades in nostalgia, but when Marty left for home to play with the Marlboros in Toronto, Gordie said, "I think those were our best days, watching the boys play, the whole family going on hockey trips. I don't guess it will ever be that way again, will it?"

It's true that you are only young twice—the youth you spend and the one you borrow from your kids. We would pile the boys and Cathy and the hockey sticks into the car and ride off for some obscure town in Canada singing made-up songs all the way. A typical lyric: "You can't get to heaven on hockey skates, 'cause you'll skate right by those pearly gates."

We did not have enough sense to worry about bad things on those trips: accidents, or mishaps, or not getting there. Once we were headed for Erie, Pennsylvania, to watch Mark and Marty play in the national tournament. The boys had to provide their own transportation, and Ed Taube, their godfather, borrowed a luxurious mobile home to take us in style. It came from his friend, the mayor of Owosso. By the time the bus pulled out, it was bulging with twelve passengers and an assortment of hockey sticks and gear. To make more room, the boys stashed their hockey bags and our suitcases in the shower stall.

As fate would have it, someone got thirsty, went to turn on the bathroom faucet, and opened the wrong spigot. The shower came on, drenching the hockey bags and the uniforms inside. We had no choice but to keep rolling. We had to make that game. Down the highway we tooled toward Erie, with wet jock straps, shin pads, and jerseys flapping out the trailer windows. People did double-takes as they passed us going the other way. We tooted the horn and waved.

Just nineteen miles outside of Erie, right on the exit ramp, the mobile home threw a rod. Flames shot out and the thing began to smoke like a fireplace with a closed damper. By now the only thing on anyone's mind was to get the boys to the stadium. I told Gord to find a way. I'd stay with the other children and the burnt-out camper. He could send someone for us later.

Can you picture it? Gordie Howe, with two kids and their hockey sticks, at the edge of the highway thumbing a ride into town. Finally, two fellows in a fastback pulled over. They couldn't believe their eyes. Here was Gordie Howe, of all things, hitchhiking to a hockey game. It must have been like spotting Arnold Palmer, with his golf bag, standing at the side of the road.

Gordie gratefully bought them a tank of gas and tried to pay them for their trouble, but they wouldn't hear of it. When he insisted, they accepted a ten-dollar bill—on condition that Gordie and the boys autograph it.

During most of those years, the boys were coached by the late Jim Chapman, a fine man who taught the fundamentals of the game well. Gordie never interfered. If Jim sought his opinion he gave it. Otherwise, he stayed out.

Growing up in the footsteps of a Gordie Howe was not always painless. The boys occasionally became the targets of fans who, in their own whimsical way, decided they had it in for Gordie. Once, when Mark was not yet seven, we drove to a Christmas tournament in Sault Ste. Marie. I was appalled, at one point, to hear the coach of the opposing team yell, "Get the lead out of your ass, Mark Howe."

For reasons I will never understand, fans asked the boys for their autographs before they were in grade school. Mark was so young he had to print his name. He did so, once, for a fan who looked at the autograph, then said right to Mark's face, "Boy, that kid of Howe's is so dumb he doesn't even know how to write his name." These cases were the exception, but they always smarted.

Even Murray, the youngest, became a minor celebrity on his first trip to a weekend tournament without Mark and Marty. The Ontario fans, kids and adults both, paid attention to him and asked for his autograph. All during the game, Murray sat on the bench, scribbling his name and pausing on occasion to yell down the line, "Hey, how do you spell *sincerely*?" His coach finally had to tell him to knock it off, but Murray was unabashed. He felt he had a major responsibility for signing autographs, inasmuch as he was the only Howe there.

In a way that wasn't clinging, Marty and Mark grew up close. Just fifteen months apart in age, often sharing rooms, they had the usual quota of fraternal disagreements. We came home one night, after Gordie had been in a grueling game, to find that our sons had gotten into a brawl—over what is no longer clear.

What was clear was the evidence of the fight. They had knocked over and shattered a twenty-gallon aquarium, drenching a carpet that had been installed only a few days earlier. Star or not, Gordie stayed up with me half the night, picking little tropical fish off the backs of furniture and sponging the carpet.

We did not often have to discipline them. Gordie says that when they discovered girls they forgot how to tell time, and he had to get on them about that. We have always felt that kids respond better to discipline than to punishment.

Marty and Mark developed a trust and loyalty that I find rare even in brothers. When it came time for Marty to think about going away to play amateur hockey in Canada, he picked the team he thought Mark would want to play with a year later. It was important to both of them to be on the same side, at least that once. They never expected, nor did we, that as professionals they would have that chance.

But they did, and since they brought their dad along with them, it made scheduling around our house a bit more unified. Even so, feeding a houseful of hockey players is like running a twenty-four-hour cafeteria. Long ago, I forgot about the normal breakfast, lunch, and dinner routine. The Howes are bacon and egg eaters, but more often than not breakfast gets skipped for morning ice practices.

We became accustomed to having our "big meal" before game time—about 1:00 P.M. The usual menu called for a sixteen-ounce porterhouse or New York strip for the guys and the Howe family's special salad, cottage cheese and pears or peaches, mixed with mayonnaise. Then it was jello or ice cream for dessert, depending on how Gordie's weight was going.

Every athlete, I suppose, has his own theory as to what he should or should not eat before a game. The menu, with an occasional rare variation, has worked for us through the years.

One year, however, my grandmother fixed Christmas dinner for the family. The Red Wings had a game that night but Gordie couldn't stand being left at home with his pregame steak. So he went to Grandma's, intending to confine himself to a taste of the turkey and a little salad.

Gordie ate like it was his last meal. Dressing. Gravy. Extra helpings of turkey. Two pieces of pie. The willpower vanished. We practically had to carry him to the car. He had only planned to stay a few minutes, make his holiday wishes, then go home to rest. By the time we left he had only thirty minutes to spare before he was due at the arena.

That night, occasionally giving his chest the old Alka Seltzer thump, Gordie scored six points—three goals and three assists. Later, he had mixed feelings about his performance. He was never one to go against training rules; it makes you feel so damned guilty. But times such as that make you wonder if the rules—the curfews, the special diets—have any merit. But I do believe that athletes need the security of a program. They may *act* irregular but they respond to order.

In our house the refrigerator is the nerve center. Especially for Marty. It's the first place Gordie and the boys head when they come home, but Marty never leaves it. He seems attached to it by some invisible cord. We always say that Marty eats just one meal a day, but it lasts from the time he gets up to the time he goes to bed.

Part of my problem is the fact that it is always feast or famine. The fellows are home for, say, eight days, the cupboards are loaded, the kitchen could feed an army. Then, suddenly, they are on the road and it's Cathy and me, and we eat out. It makes efficient grocery shopping impossible. After one road trip, I went into a grocery and came home with $194 in food. When the checker looked at the tape we both nearly fainted.

Ours is not a normal routine. On game days, the house is like a nursery. The fellows crawl into the sack for the afternoon—except for Mark, who rarely sleeps in daylight and pads quietly around the house in his socks. Gordie gets up around five P.M., dresses, and drinks tea and honey—just as he has done unfailingly for most of the last twenty-five years. In between periods, he will sip more tea, or sometimes suck on an orange. Besides containing vitamin C, the oranges are useful for the coaches to throw when they get angry. Canadians are big tea drinkers. Gord's no exception.

After the game, more often than not the boys make plans with friends or other players. Gordie, as an old married type, meets me after the game. Occasionally we go out. Most times we simply drive home, where it's nice and quiet. I'll fix us a fried-egg sandwich and bacon. Then we'll just enjoy the rest of the evening—alone.

I suppose it surprised some of their school chums and

teammates when Marty and Mark decided to live at home, even after they had signed for big money with the Aeros. I took it as a compliment. It has been fun, I think, being part of the Howe family. They have total privacy in their rooms. They are free to invite company, to come and go as they like. The only thing we forbid is entertaining female guests overnight. If they choose to do that, there are plenty of places they could go, I'm sure.

Gordie and I did decide, as a matter of policy, to charge the boys rent—room and board—of thirty dollars a week.

Mark nearly flipped when I told him. "Are you kidding?" he said. "We never had to pay anything before."

I pointed out that he wasn't making big money before. He was no longer an impoverished student. I said, "If you were a plumber now and you were out plumbing, you'd have to pay room and board. That's the way it is." But we didn't want to appear unreasonable. We offered them a choice. If they preferred, they could buy the groceries each month. Wisely, the boys agreed to pay the rent.

Mark needled me about it later, but I think he understood. The money meant nothing. But it *was* important that every member in a family complex feel that he or she was participating. It's the same as sharing the work.

And we always have shared. I have rarely had regular domestic help. We lead and always have led such public lives that I like to keep our home as private as possible. If Gord wants to walk around in his shorts, I want him to feel that he can.

We have always been do-it-yourselfers. We do a lot of our own yard work. Gordie enjoys getting into the kitchen, not to cook but to putter around. Before I know it, he's done the pans I had left soaking in the drain. This may get him drummed out of the male-chauvinist army, but Gordie Howe likes to work around the house. It's his form of relaxation.

It seems we are constantly making transitions. The fellows are home. They're gone. The pressure of the season is on. Then it's suddenly over. And you wake up one morning, and everything has come to a standstill. You don't have practice. You don't have a game. One time it's a relief, another time it's a huge letdown. Your life just stops. You wonder, "What will I do tomorrow?"

The Howe men are constantly packing and unpacking. I launder the clothes and hang them in the laundry room. They pack their own suitcases. It gets tricky trying to outguess the weather. One day they're in San Diego where the balmy breezes blow, and the next they're headed for Winnipeg where the snow is up to your armpits. When you live in Houston, you tend to forget that it's winter up north. Marty miscalculated badly after his first season. He left Houston's seventy-degree climate and stepped off the plane at Winnipeg into snow as white as the shoes he was wearing.

We have what I can only describe as a split-personality family. When Gordie and the boys return from road trips, Cathy and I have been itching to try out a nice restaurant or take in a show. They've been on the go and are ready for home-cooked meals and an evening of family bridge. Cathy and I are forced to plot constantly to get our way.

All of us, I think, take our cue from Gordie, whose capacity to relax explains at least in part his survival in a brutish sport. He can sit for hours and work crossword puzzles. He has a fine sense of his own limits and paces himself smartly. Once home, he can throw off the pressures of the game. The boys, I believe, have inherited some of that quality. I'm more active—not quite hyper but compelled to be *doing* something. We tend to balance each other nicely. His ability to relax calms me; my surges of energy help get Gordie going.

During the summer, the whole family can relax at our cottage at Bear Lake in Michigan. I bake all the fattening things we deprived ourselves of during the season. Gordie loses himself in his workshop. The boys and Cathy fish and ski. We all sail, a competition that never stops. It's always with us. We race. There is nothing I like better than beating that Number Nine sailboat.

Christmas of 1971 was spent at the lake. It was special, the first one in twenty-five years that Gordie had spent with the whole family, when he wasn't on the road or getting ready for a game that night. It was the first Christmas after his retirement. Bear Lake was covered with snow. We skied, and frolicked in the snow; our friends came by that night, stood outside on the white lawn silhouetted against the moonlight, and sang "Deck the Howes with boughs of holly."

It was the first Christmas the Howes had spent, clearly removed from an ice rink. We thought it was the beginning of a trend. But our Rink Rat days were not yet over.

It was a long walk from the Lucky Strike Bowling Alley, where Gord and I first met, to that walk down the aisle on April 15, 1953. Gord's brother Vernon is in the background.

Mark and Marty learned what hockey gear was all about at an early age. This is one of the few times Marty sported his Dad's famous Number Nine. (Detroit *News* photograph by Rolland R. Ransom)

Gord and I both laced many a pair of skates in our day. Here Gord laces Mark's while Marty and Murray (*right*) watch. I have seen a thousand kids look at Gord the way Murray is looking here. He seems to be saying, "You're my idol, too, Dad."

The boys were doing publicity shots even back in 1961-1962. Marty (*top*) Mark (*bottom*) belonged to the Teamsters and when we said that team was organized we weren't kidding. (Photographs by Dan Fodor)

Gord and I were the proud "parents" of the Grand Champion female Polled Hereford at the Michigan State Fair in 1972. Gord was almost, but not quite, as proud of that trophy as of some of those Stanley Cups. (Photograph by Snuffy McGill)

Supporting certain charities often meant more than just going door to door. Here I got into the act at a 4-H Foundation event at Michigan State University. When I wasn't quite sure what to do, the young farmer told me, "Just grab her by the tits, Mrs. Howe." (Michigan State University Information Service photograph by Robert B. Brown, used courtesy of the Michigan 4-H Foundation)

The Howe family pedaled away during a bikeathon for the March of Dimes in our Detroit suburb, Bloomfield Hills. I'm not sure that guy behind me was always doing his fair share. (Photograph by Art Emmanuel)

This is the one time the big ones didn't get away. Marty (*left*) and Mark proudly pose for this show with their dad and godfather Ed Taube. I don't know who caught what, but it looks like everyone thinks he has his fair share. (Photograph by *The Telegram*, Toronto)

Look who that guy at the left turned out to be. Arnold Palmer and Congressman Bob Griffin stand between Gordie and me and that other guy at the left—then Congressman Gerald Ford.

This was the first time the Howes played team hockey together, back in February 1971. The Detroit Red Wings took on the junior team and Gord. The game raised $30,000 for the March of Dimes. (Photograph by George Gellatly)

Then-Vice-President Spiro Agnew reads a message from President Richard M. Nixon at the official Gordie Howe retirement day in March 1972. Gordie lamented that one person was missing there all day—his mother. (Photograph by J. A. Mackey)

This was the first of many publicity shots taken for the Houston Aeros. At the time we were still the Howes of Detroit but were well on our way to becoming the Howes of Houston. *From left,* Gord, Colleen, Marty, Cathy, Murray, and Mark. (Photograph by J. A. Mackey)

This shot of the big three in blue was taken for a Howes of Houston poster. Dad's on the left with Marty (*center*) and Mark (*right*). (Photograph by J. A. Mackey)

Once he got the "old legs" back there was no stopping Gordie, who was named the W.H.A.'s most valuable player after the 1973-1974 season. (Photograph by Ed Boczon)

Marty gets congratulations from his Dad after scoring his first professional W.H.A. goal for the Houston Aeros. Marty gave me the puck after the game. Mark, Number Four, is right behind his brother. (Photograph by Sam Caldwell)

Howe and sons, Mark (*left*) and Marty (*right*), take a break in the locker room. They call their father Gordie on the ice, but at home it remains Dad. (Photograph by Sam Caldwell)

It took some getting used to—seeing the old man in blue and without a Red Wing stamped on his chest. This was taken at the W.H.A. All-Star game in Minnesota during the 1973–1974 season.

Gordie Howe, the only man in professional sports to share the same locker room with his sons, flanked by them during a face off at Sam Houston Coliseum. (Photograph by Sam Caldwell)

Mark in action during the ill-fated Team Canada Russian series in Moscow in October 1974. (Photograph by Lauri Laufman)

In front of the Kremlin Cathy and I buy flowers for three rubles from an elderly, toothless Russian woman. (Photograph by Lauri Laufman)

Gordie Howe is swamped by onlookers and autograph seekers at the GUM department store in Moscow. (Photograph by Lauri Laufman)

Marty, Cathy, and I do the sight-seeing bit in Moscow. I regret we met too many buildings and not enough people. This was taken near the grounds of the Kremlin. (Photograph by Lauri Laufman)

6
Wives and Mothers and Other Strangers

I HAD MADE UP MY MIND, had simply *willed* it, that when our first child was born his father would be there. Regrettably, babies don't read clocks, calendars, or hockey schedules. Gordie was in Boston the night our son Marty arrived.

The date was February 18, 1954. The news reached him at the end of the second period as he came off the ice to be received by his grinning teammates. The headline in the next morning's paper read: HOWES HAVE BABY; RED WINGS LOSE. The story seemed to imply, I thought, that the team shared Gordie's joy to the point of forgetting about the game.

That was all I needed. I already felt alone, unpraised, and sorry for myself. Now we—Marty and I—were being blamed for the Red Wings' defeat.

I had managed to shake off that indigo mood by the morning of the day my baby and I were to go home, which coincided, happily, with the end of the team's road trip. I couldn't wait to see Gordie and present him with his first son. I was dressed and packed and had bundled Marty when my doctor, Jim Matthews, walked in.

He was frowning. Jack Adams, Gordie's general manager, a formidable man, had called and asked Jim not to release me from the hospital. The Red Wings had a game scheduled for that night, and Jack was afraid Gordie's mind would not be on it if the baby and I came home.

I burst into tears.

Jim said, "It's all right, Colleen. I told him he could go to hell."

Interference of that kind was common in the sport twenty years ago, and among the wives it built a great resentment and a great helplessness. Much has changed since. Clubs actually welcome wives and even help them make arrangements when they move to town. But in the beginning, there was hockey. Period. Wives were to be kept separate, like your religious beliefs. The club assumed players had them, but they didn't want to know about it.

Management wanted the players to live, eat, and sleep the game. It was unheard of for them to have an outside interest—business, family, or otherwise. Teams didn't even approve of players having summer jobs. They took the position that this would divert them from thinking about the season ahead.

In reality, what took their minds off the game was just the opposite—worries about financial security, which, for most, hockey couldn't provide.

But as far as the Detroit Hockey Club was concerned, wives and winning just didn't mix. It was an attitude typical of the league and that era. Most wives simply did not feel very much a part of their husband's lives. We were seldom included in club invitations. They knew our names—they knew I was Mrs. Howe—and that was the extent of it.

The old guard at the Olympia would have croaked when they read that I helped negotiate Gordie's contract with the Aeros and that we shared an office in Houston. That would have been unheard of in the 1950s.

We were not even allowed to telephone our husbands on the road. They were free to call out, but if an emergency developed we had to call through the coach or general manager. It was one of the many practices we considered unfair and cruel, but which we accepted.

The Red Wings, even attempted to legislate our sex lives, as did most hockey clubs. Jack Adams was convinced that sex had a direct, injurious effect on a player's performance. Once the season began, Jack would tell them in blunt locker-room language, to "keep it in your pants." Jack always did have a way with words. But even pro football coaches, with their famous "Tuesday Rule"—no sex after the Tuesday before a game—didn't preach abstinence.

Wives often were blamed for losses or a particular player's slump. If the Red Wings lost and it was discovered that a player had gone grocery shopping with his wife after the team meeting that day, the conclusion was clear. The Red Wings were defeated because some spoiled and pampered wife couldn't carry her own groceries. Well, most of us had only one car, and it was pretty tough to grocery shop while your husband had it parked at the Olympia.

When the playoffs rolled around each year we took on the status of temporary widows. The Red Wings loaded the players onto a bus and whisked them away from the public—and their families—and headed for a motel hideaway outside of town. They housed them in a motel only because they couldn't find a monastery. Now, these were players who had been living at home and winning games all season. But, suddenly, the management decided they couldn't carry a hockey stick unless they had solitude. Families were persona non grata.

For the Detroit home playoff games, the team usually commuted from Toledo, Ohio, an hour's drive from Detroit.

Keep in mind that the playoffs would often stretch out for a month-and-a-half. And when Gordie finally reappeared at home, I'd practically have to say, "Hey, kids, this is no stranger, this is your father."

The idea, I suppose, was to keep them away from pesky ticket seekers, fussy children, nagging wives, and anything else that might disrupt their game. Sometimes this backfired, because the isolation would drive some of them right up the wall.

The team would stay cloistered until right before the game. Then they were bussed into the city and straight to the Olympia. After the game, of course, the bus would be waiting to take them right back to their hideaway.

If you were Gordie Howe, the autograph seekers would mob you the instant you left the locker room. And just as you'd try to break away and say hello and goodby to your wife, the bus driver would lean on his horn and yell for everyone to get on board. If I got a glimpse of Gordie's eyes or he took my hand or gave me a light kiss, that was about it.

One night, after a play-off in Detroit, Gordie stood out in the hallway signing autographs for twenty minutes—all the time he had between the dressing room and the bus. He had lost about ten pounds during the game—which was not unusual—and he was tired and weak. I was hoping we'd have a moment together, long enough to ask how he was doing and tell him about the children. But we were an ocean of people apart, because he was still on the other side of the hall, trying to satisfy everyone.

The bus driver started to honk his horn and, finally, Gordie gave everyone a small wave and moved toward the exit. One woman, furious that he was leaving without giving her son an autograph, shouted after him, "He must really think he's something. He wouldn't even sign his name for my kid."

That's when you begin to think that the windmills have won. Gordie didn't have time to say hello to his own wife or kids, and now a stranger was accusing him of having a swollen head.

There wasn't much a wife could do about being outflanked by the mob, but it didn't take us long to learn how to highstick the front office people and beat them at their own game. It took some serious conniving though.

Once, when the Red Wings were scheduled to open the play-offs at Toronto, they stashed the guys in Hamilton, Ontario. Our children's godparents, Ed and Agnes Taube (she since has died), called and invited Pat Lindsay, Ted's wife, and myself to go with them to Toronto to see the fellows.

"No way," I said. "If anyone spots us up there we'd really get Gord and Ted in trouble."

But Turkey Ed—he was in the poultry business and we always called him that—didn't take no easily, and he kept insisting we join them. Finally, I mentioned it to Gordie, who thought it was an inspired idea.

The Taubes and Pat and I located a motel just outside of Hamilton, not far from where the team was staying, but far enough. Gordie and Ted told us to go ahead and register, and somehow they'd figure a way to sneak out to see us after the game.

The desk clerk stared at Ed with what I took to be a look of suspicion when he booked a room for Agnes and himself, then separate ones for Pat and me. Ed said I was wrong. The look was one of *respect.*

We loved it. The whole arrangement was so sneaky and mischievous and scary that it seemed—well—illicit, like having an affair. We half worried, half giggled about what would happen if Jack Adams caught us. Jack ruled with an iron fist. You just didn't cross him. This fear was built into anyone connected with the Red Wings and, through it, he shaped and controlled his team for many years. But at that moment, our fear of Jack merely added to the excitement.

Gordie and Ted did sneak out and spent the night with us. I

could not face the desk clerk when they showed up the next morning to check us out of the rooms Ed had reserved for us. The clerk, of course, recognized both of them. He *knew* some hanky-panky had been going on, and he knew who was doing it.

As we left the lobby, Gordie whispered, "If you ever get an anonymous letter about my sleeping with some girl in a Hamilton hotel, you'll know it was you."

This was not the first time I had rebelled against the house rules and crossed the front office. Jack Adams publicly blasted Gordie, Ted, and another player named Marty Pavelich for going into business together in a small engineering company. Jack really laid it on. He said the fellows were making so much money, and spending so much time on business, they weren't paying attention to hockey.

His comments about the money were a joke. No one was taking a dime out of the company. And to anyone who knew Gordie, the suggestion that he could neglect hockey would be like accusing Heifetz of neglecting the violin.

I thought Jack was out of line. Feeling waspish, I called Pat Lindsay and said, "Gee, dear, I didn't know we were making all this money."

She laughed and said, "Neither did I." Whereupon the two of us decided to set the record straight.

As a put-on, we borrowed two mink stoles. I do know that neither of us had any vision of owning one in the foreseeable future. Next, we raided our monopoly sets for some spare cash and stuffed the bills into our purses.

Sitting in our seats at the Olympia that night, wrapped in fur, we lighted each other's cigarettes with our monopoly money and hammed it up for a Detroit news photographer who had spotted us. Under the photo that appeared in the next morning's paper, the caption read, "Wives Pan Adams' Comments."

The Olympia just about blew off its foundation. It took Jack a good while to forgive us for that stunt, and I'm quite sure he never forgot it. Perhaps his criticism of our husbands had been a piece of that often strange coaching psychology in which coaches attempt to inspire people by embarrassing them. I only knew that it was unfair.

The treatment of the wives was hardly surprising, in view of the fact that the teams did not even treat their players as people. They were just properties, chess pieces, and sooner or later they became trade material. Gordie was an exception in that he always had more security than most players. But for a wife, one of the most difficult adjustments was to sit back and watch how other families were shuffled around and sometimes shuffled out.

Trades are a part of the game but the timing can often be cruel, and the insensitivity behind them makes you want to scream. Such a time was the winter Billy McNeill's wife died of polio during her eighth month of pregnancy. Joan had been buried only a week, and Billy was in the throes of caring for a young daughter and still in shock when the Detroit club traded him. I couldn't believe it. No trade could have been that urgent.

I was never able to handle lightly the news that friends— we thought of the wives, too—had been traded. You saw it and felt it in human terms when you knew the people, how dedicated they were, what problems they had. I suppose that was why general managers make it a point not to fraternize with the players. When it came to the team, personal welfare and feelings were incidental.

The wife of a hockey player learned to live year by year. There were no long-term contracts. Gordie, like the others, knew that each year was a clean slate, and each year could be his last. There were no cushy four- or five-year contracts then, no guaranteed salary payments in cases of crippling injuries.

Of course, no job offers total security, with the possible exception of a seat on the U.S. Supreme Court. But if one was, for example, an accountant and did his job well, he usually didn't need a contract to keep it. But in hockey, frequently, the better you performed the more likely you were to be traded. Not the superstars, but the not-quite-great and the fringe people—they were watched for improvement like calves being fattened for eventual sale.

Under such conditions, wives and children led a necessarily transient existence. The rumors often were as difficult to endure as the trades themselves. When things went badly for the club, the instinct of management under pressure for their own jobs was to fire the coach or tear up the roster. The owners were yelling. The public was yelling. Rumors flew and trades started.

In Detroit the hockey player and his family were the last to know about a trade. They would read about it in the paper, or be informed by a friend who had heard it on the radio. Or they would just get a call from the trainer for the player to come pick up his skates. No one was told why or how, only that he was gone—out.

So he picked up his skates and waited for a call from the new club. If the new team was on the road he would join the squad there, leaving his wife to pack, check the kids into a new school, and look for another home. The Howes were lucky—we went through only one trade rumor and it, obviously, was unfounded.

This was why players and their families were so grateful to get two or three years in the same city. Even in the seventies, with the longer contracts made popular by the hockey war, there were no guarantees against a player being traded. You could count on one hand those who had enough leverage to command a no-trade clause. So, basically, it was still a rootless occupation.

Slowly, the clubs have started to join the twentieth century; they have begun to recognize the wife and family. I even saw the chauvinistic Detroit Red Wings institute some changes. For years, the wives had no place to entertain guests before and after the game. Finally, we were given memberships to the private clubrooms at the Olympia. We paid our own bar and food bills, of course, but the membership brought us in out of the halls.

Traditions do not die easily, even among those who have been injured by them. The new policy offended Gloria Abel, whose husband, Sid, had begun his Detroit career in 1938 and was now the general manager. Gloria told Edna Gadsby that standing out in the hall had been good enough for her all the years that Sid was playing, and it ought to be good enough for the current wives. It was as if letting us into the private rooms represented a lowering of the standards.

As the years went by there were fewer stag affairs for the athletes, and the old custom of seating the wives at a separate table amost disappeared. In other years, you were lucky if you got a ticket to get in.

In 1972 Cathy and I were among the first women to be invited to the National Hockey Hall of Fame dinner—to watch Gordie's induction. The family of Bernie (Boom Boom) Geoffrion, Montreal's colorful scorer, was also able to attend. Such occasions had always been considered For Men Only, and trying to change that was like trying to desegregate the Masonic Lodge. Clarence Campbell, the only president the league had known since 1946, was responsible for the new policy, and the Howes were grateful to him.

It was important to Gordie that his family be there to see him inducted into the society of hockey's immortals. That families were ever denied this pleasure was and is a mystery to me.

Although they reacted rudely at times, management as a

general rule was correct in recognizing the influence of the hockey wife on her husband's career. She had the capacity to make things very good, or to make them impossible—for him, for her, and for his future.

Instead of trying to stamp them out, hide them, keep them out of sight like a retarded uncle, the clubs could have enlisted the wives as willing allies. It was once unheard of for the player's lady to attend an out-of-town game. If she went, she did so as a private citizen, without courtesies. If she were so much as seen in the hotel where the team was staying, the player would catch hell. It was taboo.

Obviously, you can't have a bunch of wives traveling with the team. But it would be a smart and thoughtful gesture if all the wives were asked to accompany them on, say, one designated road trip. It has never been done, but I expect it to be a part of many changes to come.

Besides proving that the club has a heart and providing a special weekend for the player and his wife, it might serve one very important psychological purpose. It would show the wives that road trips are not as glamorous and glorious as they seem when you're the one sitting at home, listening to the kids yowl and waiting for the plumber.

Road trips—at one time or another—are the bugaboo of every hockey marriage.

From the start, I knew I was going to be spending large chunks of time alone. I made up my mind: Either I was going to spend it being miserable or I was going to fill those hours and do something useful. I am not the kind who enjoys traditional, pre-lib women's activities—bridges and teas. So most of the early years revolved around the children and working with their hockey programs or Cathy's Blue Bird troop. As our income grew, I became more involved in running the financial affairs of the family. And along the way I worked with a number of charities, as did all the Howes.

But even when one keeps busy, the adjustment to a husband who is away half the time isn't easy. There were many moments when you ached for someone to share the joys and disappointments that came, but he wasn't *there*. Once in a while you cursed him for the heartless brute he was. But you went back to cooking the kids' supper and you coped, alone. It made you extremely independent. Hopefully, it made you a little more mature.

And because Gordie and I were not together more often, we had to learn to share certain things independent of each other. This I learned the hard way.

When Gordie passed Maurice Richard as the National Hockey League's all-time leading scorer, it was, at the time, probably the biggest milestone of his career. The team, wouldn't you know, was on the road when it happened. So there I sat, at home, feeling sorry for myself. I didn't feel a part of it. Not only that, I resented a fate that always kept the wives away on nights when their husbands distinguished themselves. Poor Gordie. He had achieved this spectacular goal, and his wife was so busy enjoying her own misery she couldn't be happy for him.

While I was moping about the house with all my mixed emotions, thinking these pitiful thoughts, the doorbell rang. A delivery boy handed me a bouquet of mixed flowers, in a long-stemmed blue goblet, from Fran Lynch—whose husband broadcast the Red Wings' games. A note was attached. "To the gal behind the whole thing. I know Gordie is being honored by so many people today. I just wanted to congratulate you on what you have contributed to his success."

That note turned me around. My spirits soared, and I was reminded again that one of the hardest lessons in marriage is not to take yourself too seriously.

Of course, it is much more complicated than just the loneliness of a moment. What upsets the sports wife and lies beneath the surface of some of her anxiety, is the question of what her husband does off the ice, on the road.

Here's how the problem usually begins. Sooner or later, a wife sees an opposing player with a strange companion, while his team's playing in her town. It is a whole new world, and suddenly it occurs to her, "What is my husband doing when I'm not there?"

You find out that girls actually call your husband's room and invite themselves up; some are brazen enough to just knock at the door. I know for a fact that this is not a rarity. You discover firsthand that it's there for the asking.

These girls are called "groupies." In an earlier, less sophisticated time, we had another name for them. Whatever one calls them, they can be found hanging around the lobbies and the bars in each town where the fellows go after a game. Married or single, a player has every opportunity for a little casual romance.

To these gals, I think the athletes symbolize physical men living in a public world. It's sad that so few of them understand just how temporary the players' interest is. They are half-forgotten the moment they are half-loved. I don't know of any player who ever left his wife for any of these women, even if the affair was a long one. In fact, you rarely heard of a hockey divorce, certainly not in the fifties.

For the athlete, these encounters were often the result of loneliness or pressure or a sagging ego. But as far as I was concerned, this was where you separated the men from the boys—those who were willing to jeopardize their marriages and possibly their careers.

It surprised me that the fellows who did get deeply involved with their casual ladies failed to foresee the consequences. Sometimes the girl fell in love, and because she had the player's full attention when he came to town, she persuaded herself that he would leave his family. These affairs always ended unhappily, often angrily, with a nasty letter from the rejected girl being received by the player's wife. This happened to more than one unlucky guy.

If sex was needed or desired by a player, it was always available. As a wife, you just had to reassure yourself that your husband loved you and the rest didn't matter. You had to learn control. Otherwise you couldn't lead that kind of life —at least, not happily.

No woman ever made the error of making a pass at Gordie in my presence. But Gordie—and I don't mean to set him apart—doesn't have, and never did have, the lover-boy or rounder image. But I'm not naive. During our marriage he has probably had a good look at someone else. For all I know, he may have had an affair or two. What I do know is how deeply Gordie cares about me and the rest of his family. With this I feel secure.

Should I sound more morally indignant or alarmed about the threat that exists out there? I'm sorry. Mary Poppins doesn't live here any more. This is the real world. What is right and moral and just are still the essential virtues, but people do not always define them in the same way. Times change. People change. Today you see young girls doing *on* the stage what they used to do off the stage—so they could get on stage. We are not so easily shocked any more.

If a wife is around long enough, she begins to see past the hustling females. She realizes that travel isn't wild and glamorous, but an exercise in tedium. Much of the time is spent waiting around airports. Traveling with a team isn't quite the same as a vacation with the family. You have to be at the airport a boring hour-and-a-half to two hours before flight time so all the equipment can get loaded. Almost a hurry-up-to-wait sort of schedule.

Then they hang around the hotel lobbies. That much never changes. Except for the rookies and the younger ones who are turned on by new cities and new sounds and filled with discovery, athletes are among the world's great lobby sitters. After a time they take on the look of those old men who sit on a bench at a bus stop, dozing, never getting on.

They simply can't raise hell on a regular basis and keep up the pace of modern pro sports. On game days they usually have a quick breakfast, a light workout, a meeting, a pregame meal, and then they rest until it's time to leave for the arena. They are under constant pressure—on the road for two or three weeks at a time, on an emotional roller coaster of wins and losses and so much of the time just bored and lonely.

For the wife of a superstar—I dislike that overworked word but it is descriptive—there is the added problem of rescuing what is left of your own ego. You begin to feel like a shadow, a nonentity. Frequently, we'd walk into a room and everyone would grab Gordie. I'd be left standing there like one of the potted palms, wondering if anyone would notice that I was there. They usually do, after a while.

Some wives either got used to standing alone, feeling invisible, or they handled it by hitting the bar. I had to work consciously to make sure this kind of thing didn't build resentment within me. After all, I reminded myself, it wasn't Gordie's fault. He tried to see that it didn't happen, but often he would simply get swept away by a human wave.

I had to come to terms with my feelings—I could either get bitter or work against it. I knew what I meant to Gordie and thus did not feel unappreciated. I could watch him on the ice, feel the pride surge within me at what he was doing, and yet truly believe that I had a role in his success. That was my defense. Even so, I didn't always handle it gracefully.

Once, Gordie and I and the group from Bear Lake attended a dinner honoring Duffy Daugherty, then the football coach at Michigan State, at the Owosso Country Club. A poolside cocktail party at the home of a doctor and his wife preceded the dinner. We walked in and, instantly, Gordie was whisked away. I was left standing in the foyer, while the hostess excitedly told each new arrival that Gordie Howe was at her party. Much later she bumped into me and said, "I'm sorry. I would have introduced you, but I didn't know your name."

"My name is Mrs. Howe," I said, rather coolly.

I knew she was trying to excuse her bad manners by saying she didn't know my first name, but my irritation surfaced. I shouldn't have done that because my reaction flustered her, and she clearly felt squelched. I had repaid rudeness with rudeness. I since have forgotten her name, too.

For a hockey mother, the problems tended to be less self-centered. They were more related to the lioness protecting her cubs. I thought almost constantly about Marty, Mark, and Murray. It wasn't just the hectic scheduling—you grew used to that threat. But there were other matters, such as school and their sense of priority. Athletes, whether they play football, hockey, or tennis, carry a special burden. Their practices and games demand so much of their time it is difficult not to let the studies slip, much less lead what others might consider a *normal* childhood. We tried to see that as far as our boys were concerned, hockey did not become their universe. Except for an occasional Gordie Howe, hockey is not a lifetime career. Most are lucky to get seven good years out of the sport.

After a Marlboro game Marty once had to interrupt an interview with a sportswriter to take a long distance call from his dad. The high school in Toronto had called to tell us Marty had skipped his classes that day. He must have looked fairly shaken when he put down the phone because the reporter instinctively put away his note pad and suggested they postpone the interview.

"Rough, huh?" the writer said, sympathetically.

Marty nodded. "And when my dad got through with me," he grimaced, "my *mother* got on the phone."

Marty graduated, despite all the adjustments he had to

make that first year in Canada — a new family, a new school environment, a new hockey team. We were proud of him. Mark, however, left school the next year and still needed two credits to get his high school diploma when he signed with Houston. We had some serious, even emotional talks about this. Mark has an exceptional mind. He was always an honor student. The irony was that Gordie, at times, has felt inadequate because of his lack of formal education. He makes no bones about it when he speaks to youth groups.

I believed that both boys were cheating themselves by not being in college, or at least attending class part-time. We let the issue ride in that hectic first year after the move to Houston. The boys had enough pressure on them. But I was sure the time would come when they would realize the need for more education. In today's society, I believe you need all you can get, short of physical pain.

Murray is the family intellectual, an all-A honor student. I have hoped that he might play college hockey and continue his studies. At fifteen, of course, his sights were on following after his father and big brothers. There will be even heavier pressure on Murray, and I think about that. It's a bigger challenge for him since Marty and Mark have already made it. They have qualified as pros and are playing better all the time.

On a television show one night, in 1973, a psychic predicted our futures. She told us much of what was obvious, but then announced that Murray would become the most successful of the Howes. But not in hockey, in journalism. Murray was outraged. No one was going to tell him he wouldn't be the next professional hockey player in the Howe family.

Murray's letters from Detroit indicated what was in his mind and heart. Often they came addressed to The Howe Family Minus One:

> Dear Mom and Dad,
> You have just been chosen as the lucky couple to buy the enclosed tickets. These

fantastic high quality raffle tickets for my hockey team are yours to buy, but just for being picked you get free—yes, free—these pictures of your son in action on the ice and in front of the school camera, plus two pieces of cardboard. Tell Cathy to get her tonsils fixed and Dad to get the Aeros winning.

Your Gifted Son,
Murray.

Murray is the creative one in the family. We knew he could talk his way out of anything after he wrote his own father a "hate" letter. When Murray was small, he misbehaved in such a way as to bring down the wrath of his father. After a lecture he marched downstairs and asked me for Gordie's address at the rink. The request puzzled me, but I gave it to him. A few days later Gordie came home with his latest batch of mail, and one of the envelopes was addressed in what looked strangely like Murray's penmanship. Gordie opened it and read the following:

Dear Dad,
I do not like you.

Love,
Murray

When Gordie confronted him with the letter, Murray's face turned red. He had already forgotten why he was mad. He looked at the letter as if it were in code. Then he brightened.

"Don't you get it, Dad?" he asked. "I don't like you—I *love* you." We have since decided that Murray will be the politician in the family.

7
The Game They Play

I HAD BAD VIBES about that night—a feeling you can't explain, like knowing a storm is coming. Marty was tired, he had been feeling puny for two weeks, and over the phone I tried to coax him into coming home early for the holidays.

But Marty wouldn't hear of it. The Russians were coming. The Marlboros had one more game, against an offshoot of the Soviet Olympic team, and he insisted on playing. It was a commitment he wanted to keep.

Although we didn't know it then, in the fading days of 1973, this was to be our last Christmas in Detroit. It would also be Marty's last game as an amateur, but we didn't know that, either. He was coming down with mononucleosis.

Gordie and I drove to Toronto to see the game and bring the boys home. We took our seats in the Maple Leaf Gardens, next to Dick and Rita Tanner, the couple with whom the boys boarded in Canada, and we soaked up that special excitement that international matches, at any level, always create.

Midway through the game the Russians controlled the puck and moved into the Marlboro zone. Marty went behind the net. A Russian swooped in from the other side. Marty had his head down—a grave mistake, something you *never* do. The Russian came up with his stick—the old behind-the-net technique where not everything is seen.

The stick split Marty's lip and sent him reeling into the ice. He struggled to his feet. His head hanging, his hand against his mouth, he skated directly to the bench, something I had never seen him do. Angrily, he threw off his gloves.

Blood ran down his chin and splattered his blue and white jersey. My eyes never left him. I knew Marty was hurt—badly, I feared. As I watched him leave the ice my stomach churned. Only the Christmas before, Marty had spent the entire holiday in the hospital, having a fractured cheekbone wired.

That night Gordie had sat by his bed, telling him, "This is part of hockey, son. It's not all fun and glory."

I was convinced from looking at him that Marty would be spending another unpleasant holiday. I *knew* that scattered out behind that damned net was a mouthful of my son's teeth. To a hockey wife and/or mother, teeth are more precious than diamonds. No stranger can fully appreciate the joy we feel at seeing a child smile with teeth that are his own. We carry on the way rich ladies do about missing pieces of Wedgwood china.

If Marty did have any teeth left in his mouth, I knew they must be broken off, and that would require oral surgery. I expected the worst.

I had spent hours after games with Gordie when he needed dental work. I'd seen his mouth so swollen he could barely sip soup through a straw. I had visions of Marty spending another holiday with his jaw wired and I couldn't face it—after all he had suffered in the past year. They had wired his cheekbone in three places.

Rita Tanner knew I was coming apart at the seams. She turned to me and said, "Maybe Mark knows. If I can catch his attention perhaps he can tell us if Marty is all right."

Years of experience taught you that wives and mothers didn't rush to the bench or to the dressing room. You waited for someone to bring you the word, or a sedative.

Rita caught Mark's eye, motioned to him, and pointed to her teeth, a gesture that clearly asked, "How many did he lose?"

Mark flashed back all five fingers.

That did it. I was angry and an emotional wreck. I had to get out of the stands before 12,000 people saw what a crybaby Marty's mother was. I made a beeline for the empty pressroom down the hall. I cried my eyes out, making up for all the times I bit my lip to keep from crying. The more I thought of Marty and his five missing teeth, the harder I cried.

At that moment I would have traded the entire sport of ice hockey for an empty gum wrapper. How much, I asked myself, can one kid take? Why did he have to play this stupid game? Why were stitches and facial wires and knee surgery always a part of our lives? Who needs this?

I could picture what was going on back in the locker room, the pain Marty must be feeling. I could see him clutching the edges of the table as they worked on him.

When Mark was ten or eleven, I watched a doctor stitch his lip after he had taken a stick across the mouth. As I waited for word about Marty, that memory of Mark kept flashing back to me.

The doctor had injected several needles into his upper lip to deaden the pain. Then he threaded a long, curved needle. I kept trying to talk to Mark to take his mind off the procedure. But I only jabbered while my eyes were glued to his hands gripping the table. Hanging on. Not a word. Not a tear. And the doctor kept yanking the curved needle through the flesh and drawing up the stitches. Mark's lip resembled a bloody toadstool. I turned hot, then cold. I could feel my knees buckling.

Finally, Mark took a long, slow look at me and said, "Mother, this is hurting you a lot more than me. I'm okay. I don't think it's good for you to watch. Why don't you go outside and I'll be out in a minute?"

Just a ten- or eleven-year old boy-man, sending his stricken mother from the room.

While all this was tumbling through my mind, Carl Brewer, who had once played with Gordie in Detroit, wandered into the pressroom. He couldn't believe it.

"Colleen," he said, "I've never seen you like this before. You've been through much worse. Do you want me to check on Marty?"

I was still trying to compose myself long enough to answer Carl, when Gordie walked in. He had just come from the locker room. He put his arm around me and said, "It's all right. Marty's going to be all right."

Between sobs I said, "How can he be all right with five teeth missing? How much bad luck can one kid take?"

Gordie looked puzzled. He grabbed my hand. "Come on," he said, "I'll show you."

He marched me right past the doorman and into the locker room. There sat Marty—no broken jaw, no teeth missing, only five stitches sewn into his lip. Facial cuts, of course, bleed profusely and often look much worse than they are. Trying to feel the damage, the player can smear the blood until he looks like something out of a vampire movie. All this I knew, should have known, but in the weakness of the moment had ignored.

Mark, aware Marty was okay and not realizing how upset I would be, had been teasing. Marty looked up at me, saw I had been crying, and said very gently, "But, Mom, I'm okay."

"Well, your brother is not okay," I joked. "He's going to have five of *my* fingers in *his* mouth when I get hold of him."

You live and die, your stomach turns cartwheels, as you watch the men in your life skate. You see them bashed into the boards, see sticks slapped across their mouths, and you have to learn to accept it as a hazard of the job. Test pilots, steeplejacks, bullfighters, race drivers—they accept the risks as part of the overhead of working at something that pleases them. The wife learns to keep a stiff upper lip, to put up a front for the guys, for the younger children in the family, and for the public. Otherwise, she becomes a basket case.

Hockey leaves an imprint, there's no doubt. Gordie has had so much surgery he looks like a patchwork quilt. Both knees. Elbows. Hernia. Concussion. He tore a rib cartilage once in Boston, an injury so painful he could hardly breathe. He has endured 500 stitches, which some say qualifies him for the *Guinness Book of Records*. Gordie has been lucky with his teeth—only a few are missing. While most men his age worry over receding hairlines, hockey players worry about receding teeth. Many of them have a complete set of dentures by their thirtieth birthdays.

Gordie is one of those people blessed with a high threshhold of pain. One night his teeth were jammed up into his gums when a stick caught him flush across the mouth. The black tape marks were still on his teeth. After the game we went to the office of Dr. Muske, the Red Wings' dentist, and he worked on Gordie until the small hours of the morning. Gordie never said a word the entire time.

When we finally walked out of the office, he said, "How about a cold beer?"

Often they stitch players without freezing them. Right after the cut is incurred, the area is deadened by the impact of the puck or stick. Gordie says the nerves in the triangle in your face—around the nose, below the mouth—make you hit the ceiling when stitches are needed there. But in areas such as the forehead, where there are not many nerve endings, it is hardly more painful than getting your ears pierced.

By and large, athletes have a well-defined sense of gallows humor. That is, they can usually find some reason to laugh during the unlikeliest moments of pain and anguish. Gordie does have a hairline that has lost valuable ground over the years.

Whenever he would get a head slash and the physician would start shaving, Gordie would implore him, "Not too much, Doc. I'm trying to save what's left."

Gordie's impish humor did get the goat of one doctor, during a time when he was laid up with an injured knee. While we were waiting for the team physician, Dr. Karibo, who had read the original x-rays, dropped in and asked Gordie how the knee was doing. Without waiting for an answer he decided to see for himself and examined it at length, flexing, poking, twisting, squeezing, and bending the limb.

"I can't believe how well this knee has responded," he marveled. "You should be able to play tomorrow."

"That's great," said Gordie, drily, "but you have the wrong knee."

The doctor just shook his head. "Gordie Howe," he said, "you're going to get yours. The next time you come in here . . ." And he walked out, still mumbling to himself.

Mouth injuries are a special kind of torture. They fester and often lead to other problems. Every time Gordie got hit in the mouth he would end up with dime-sized canker sores. If you had stitches on one side of the inside of the mouth you had to chew on the other side. For a broken jaw physicians removed the teeth, wired the jaws shut, and then told the player to live on liquids for as long as it took to mend.

The improvement in the care and medical attention teams give their players has been one of the major changes in hockey. In Gordie's early years he sometimes walked to the hospital for treatment after a game. Years ago, in fact, the trainer was often just a hockey player who suddenly got a job taping ankles. He didn't necessarily have the technical knowledge or the background that most trainers have today.

Gordie regarded the trainer in Houston, Bobby Brown, as the best he's played under. It made him, and it made me, feel more secure knowing the players were being cared for by a solid professional. The trainer is a key figure on any team, not only the link between the player and the doctor, but at times their resident cheerleader and psychologist.

Knowing how it once was, it came as a mild shock in later years to read the team directories in the press guide and see listed there not just one, but a team of physicians and a team dentist.

In the old school, the fellows played no matter how seriously they might be injured. Yet the worst thing they could do to a hockey player was to put him on the bench. In the days before television, they actually used to stop a game so the goalie could get a face full of stitches, then return to the ice. It did beat sitting in the dressing room, I suspect, with a swollen mouth and no sympathy except your own.

I have seen Gordie play with a fever of 102 degrees. A business executive wouldn't dream of going to the office with a fever like that.

I've seen Gordie play with a broken foot, seen him leave a hospital after passing a painful kidney stone and that night score four or five points—a typical Howe comeback. His remedy has always been to either skate it off or shake it off. He has taught his sons that pain is part of the game, and the only one who hasn't finally adjusted to it is his wife.

During one week in March of 1974, Mark pulled a back muscle, Marty hurt his shoulder, and Gordie had a cast covering a broken bone in his foot. Then came a call from Detroit from the lone holdout, Murray. He was calling to report that he had taken a shot in the mouth and his braces had cut his gums and lip.

"Join the club, Murray," I said.

When I hung up the phone, I turned and glared at the other fellows lounging around the family room. "This togetherness," I announced, "is going a little too far."

When you have seen the scarred faces and the neck harnesses, and you know the blood on their shirts is their own, you begin to understand what dishing it out means. You understand about protecting yourself, about being tough and aggressive. And you can understand Gordie Howe's philosophy: It is always better to give than to receive.

This is the golden rule by which Gordie abides on the ice. He *always* keeps his word. If a player gets a chunk out of him, Gordie will say quietly, evenly, "You've got one coming." And he delivers.

It is a peculiar sensation to hear the gentle man who sleeps beside you described as a dirty player. I can answer that just as soon as someone defines it for me. What is dirty to some may be colorful to others. I have read that Gordie has, or had, the fastest elbows in hockey, elbows like knives, and that he shaded the rules and faked out officials with his innocent, "Who me?" look. Some say that playing against Gordie was like skating through a concrete mixer.

While Gordie never won the Lady Byng award for sportsmanship, I can't believe that anyone who knew him or played alongside him would ever describe him as a dirty player. Tough, competitive, aggressive, indelicate—those designations I can accept. It's true that he did break the nose of New York's Lou Fontinato in a now famous confrontation in Madison Square Garden years ago. But no one ever accused him of taking a cheap shot at an opponent. I don't believe he was vicious or ruthless.

Once, when the Montreal goalie, Gump Worsley, lay

helpless on the ice after a sprawling save, the puck was loose in front of his face. Gordie could have rifled a shot that would surely have produced a goal, the only problem being that he might have taken Gump's nose with it. He fell on the puck to stop the play and protect the opposing goalie.

"Thanks, pal," said Worsley, as he got to one knee.

"Forget it," said Gordie, with a shrug. "I'll get another chance."

If anyone wished to keep score, the record would show clearly that Gordie has been dealt far more injuries, been in many more hospitals, and suffered countless more stitches than those who were on his receiving end.

Throughout his career he was a marked man, a moving target. A scoring champion not only has to prove himself with the puck every night, he must always be aware that he is the one in the other team's gunsight. If you slow down the big threat, the theory goes, you slow down the team.

When Gordie made his first road swing with the Aeros, Carl Brewer, who by then was with the Toronto Toros, was quoted as saying, "Gordie Howe is the dirtiest hockey player who ever lived."

Gordie didn't flinch. "I guess poor Carl is mad," he said, "because he had a bad night."

The fact is that Gordie was often counted among those who were known as *policemen,* because they kept the game honest. In hockey you have to establish a code of reprisal: If someone takes a crack at you, he has to pay for it. At least, you do if you want to last twenty-five years.

Mark Mulvoy, of *Sports Illustrated,* once asked one of Gordie's Houston teammates, a fine young forward named Frank Hughes, to describe Gordie's style.

"When the rest of us get the puck," he said, "there are always a couple of opponents ready to whack us, knock us down, and take it away. But when Gordie gets it, they clear out. Cripes, he gets twenty or thirty feet of room. The players know he didn't survive all those years by playing cute."

I know from personal reference that Gordie resents being called dirty. He was furious when a joking remark made by Mark to a friend—"I knew my dad was an old man, but I didn't know he was a *dirty* old man"—appeared in print, quoted seriously. He growled some more when a blurb on the cover of a Canadian news magazine called him "Hockey's Mean Old Man." In the Aeros locker room there were knowing grins.

"That's Gordie," said one, "and it always will be Gordie. That is why he's great."

Though they idolized their dad's toughness, we never taught our children meanness. We tried to make sure they understood the meaning of fair play. We learned early that we had to be careful what we said. Back when Mark was still a preschooler, he ran breathlessly into our first home on Stawell Avenue one day and said, "Some boy is picking on Marty."

Gordie, not realizing little Mark was going to take him seriously, said, "Well, you're not going to let someone beat up on your big brother, are you? Why don't you clunk him over the head with a hockey stick?"

That was all the encouragement Mark needed. He grabbed the first stick he saw—in our house there were always some from which to make a choice—and raced back out the door. Out of the corner of his eye Gordie saw him flash through the hall. He quickly put down whatever he was reading and hightailed after him. He got there just in time to stop Mark from clobbering the kid.

Though we quarreled and scuffled among ourselves like any family, the Howes were quick to come to the aid of a member in distress, real or imagined. If anybody wanted to take on one

Howe, he had to contend with them all. There is a lot of love in our family, and this is one place where it showed.

Typically, our boys glorified the fighting that was so often a part of hockey games. This came through in a fan letter nine-year-old Mark wrote his dad in March of 1964.

> Dear Daddy,
> We had practis at 7 in the mornin. Mrs. V. drove us to the skateing club. Thursday we are going to bramton. If you win the Stanly Cup we will win in bramton. i am glad you beat up the man in Chicago. He could not beat you up if he tried. i hope you have a happy birtheday.
> Sincerely,
> Mark Howe

Gordie had objected to the appearance of a drunken fan on the team bus after a play-off game. When the fellow got obnoxious, Gordie handed his tote bag to a teammate and flattened the intruder with one punch. The story made the evening news. In expressing his admiration for his father, I always felt that Mark showed a nice touch of restraint: "Sincerely, Mark Howe."

Having been exposed to the sport almost from birth, the boys learned sooner than most the value of one hockey quality—control. Gordie used to watch Marty and groan, "Oh, Christ, Marty, don't take after that guy." But all young hockey players go through this, the urge to bang people around when it isn't necessary. Looking back, Gord called himself a dogcatcher: "I went after everything that ran." The plus factor is that you can't teach a player to hit. It comes as instinct.

After Gordie's first few games in 1946, Jack Adams had accused him of trying to take on the entire N.H.L. He spent more time in the penalty box than he did on the ice. But rookies tend to be feisty. They have early pressure on them, and they can get noticed in two ways: by scoring goals or by fighting. Gordie tried too hard, at the outset, to make his name the second way. But he had a lot at stake. The New York Rangers had rejected him in an earlier training camp. He was fighting for his future. If he didn't make it, he'd have to go back to Saskatoon and bring in the wheat crops.

Hockey's critics have called the sport brutal, the action sometimes barbaric, the players animals. That characterization is simply not fair or true.

We have heard a great deal about violence in movies, on television, and in sports. Cathy and I went to see a movie, not considered very sensational, called *Walking Tall,* the story of a southern sheriff who fought against mob interests and organized rackets. The audience was practically on its feet applauding as heads were being bashed in. It nearly made me ill. But people obviously love these gruesome films, and they are not all that different when it comes to sports.

How many go to enjoy the clash of skills, and how many to see the brush with injury or near-death, I can't say. I do not think of hockey as a brutal game. The cases of deliberate injury, of a player coming up from behind and cracking another player on the head, *trying* to maim him, are rare and well documented.

Hockey players have their own code of ethics. If there are players who want blood—and there are some—they will eventually be sorted out. That is why they have rules and officials. The fellow who wants to make a reputation by seriously injuring someone is going to spend time in the penalty box. What the rules miss, the club policemen will pick up.

Of course, Amy Vanderbilt doesn't make the rules. They will work on an injured player's weakness, which is one reason teams hesitate to reveal such information to the press. They are not eager to let the opposition know that someone has a bum right knee.

When Gordie played with that arthritic condition in his left wrist, in his last seasons with Detroit, he had to compensate by handling the puck and stick almost solely with his right hand. The other players knew he had this weakness. If they took a good crack at his right wrist, when it was the only healthy one he had, it was part of their job. They aren't trying to disable you, but they do nibble away. You get the spearing in regions where you don't have much protection. That's part of the game, too.

The speed and action of hockey normally keep you on the edge of your seat. It is no game for a player who fears being hit or who waits to see what is going to happen to him next. Gordie calls them snow throwers.

"There is no such thing as a scared hockey player," I have heard him say. "But some of them are, well, cautious. If you get one like that—a snow thrower—you can run at him a few times and see where he's going to throw the puck, then you've got a little edge on him. You find your snow throwers by trial and error. If you run at the wrong man, he'll throw a spear through you."

Gordie meant someone like Blackjack Stewart, a legendary Detroit defenseman, who seldom came out of his own end of the ice. But he dared anyone to come into it.

One day, Gord picked up his stick and said, "My God, Jack, how do you ever shoot with this piece of lumber?"

Stewart said, "You don't; you break arms with it."

Today the game is designed for speed and stamina. You have to be in peak condition just to skate, much less play hockey.

I have watched, with Gordie, not only the style but the attitudes of the game change. There is less personal rivalry today. Back when the teams rode trains, some of the Detroit players wouldn't go through the dining car if they thought some of the Toronto or Montreal players would be there. Even I wouldn't have been caught dead talking to an opposing player after a game. Now, if an old friend—that's a rival you've known so long there is no anger left—is in town, we invite him over to the house after the game. Other families do the same for the Howes.

It used to be that when there were only six teams in the league and they were playing each other all the time, it was easier to keep the fires stoked. Some of the fellows kept their vendettas going for an entire career. Now, if someone gets a piece of your hide late in the season, you may not see him again until next year, unless your teams reach the play offs.

Gordie's anger was of a detached, calculated kind. He did not have a short fuse but on at least one occasion he did blow up for what he thought was just cause. Gordie was then, in the late fifties, having a problem with blinking his eyes, which we assumed was the result of his head injury. Later, the doctors decided that it may have been caused by a virus. Over the years it largely cleared up, recurring only during periods of heavy stress. But Gordie has always been a proud man, and he resented being teased or taunted. Opposing fans would sometimes call him "Blinky," a sure way to raise his temper.

During one face off the opposing player looked Gordie straight in the eye and kept blinking at him. At that moment you could have lighted a cigarette on Gordie's neck. He didn't like being mocked. The first chance he got he spread that luckless fellow onto the boards like apple butter.

One of the fellow's teammates leaned over and said, "Why the hell did you do that?"

"I don't like the idea of being mocked," Gord snapped.

He learned later that the other player also had an eye affliction. And if ever in his career Gordie Howe felt guilty about taking a chunk out of someone, it was The Blinker.

I have mixed emotions about the frequency of fights in hockey. I don't approve, but I understand them. An elbow to the mouth can ruin a fellow's disposition, and he carries his anger with him. There is no time or place to drop it off. Sometimes a good, healthy fight clears the air. It stops some of the intimidation. At times a player simply has to say, "I've had it." And the gloves go down.

What really alarms me is when the benches empty and, worse, when the crowd gets into it, I object to the too-frequent fights mainly because they too easily overshadow the game itself. I have seen slow-motion films of hockey that begged to be set to music. The skaters moved like a line of poetry. When you see how really graceful they are under these intense conditions, you appreciate the skill of the players. They need eyes in the backs of their heads to know where the opponent is, to move the puck, and avoid being hit. The action is constant and spontaneous.

Hockey has provided the Howes with a great and honest living. Gordie has been able to experience a career unparalleled in sports. Hockey will always be a part of our world.

We know that Mark and Marty will suffer their moments of aggravation simply because they are the sons of Number Nine. They already have. But we have tried to instill in them the idea that the surest way to silence such people is to put the puck in the net. If you lose control, you take your mind off the game. For the most part, their talent and being fortunate enough to play on good teams in winning seasons has kept the criticism to a tolerable level.

But one night at a game outside Windsor, the first puck hadn't even been dropped when a fan started yelling at them, "Your old man stinks and you do, too."

Just two feet away, Marty never looked up. The heckler was just getting into his act. His comments came faster and cruder. The next thing I knew, Marty had scored from the point. Then Mark scored. Then Marty again. Now Mark. The heckler got up and stomped out of the rink as the fans in his area, all picking up on the little drama, began to ride him unmercifully.

Mom Howe hasn't always taken her own advice. More than one obnoxious fan has felt the swat of my program across his face or smarted from an unexpected tongue lashing.

Years ago, when Pat Lindsay and I were sitting together in Detroit, both of us very pregnant, a drunk sitting directly behind us slurred out obscenities by the handful, the way most fans eat popcorn. I bit my tongue throughout the first period. Then another fan asked him to knock it off.

"Have you no decency?" he said. "After all, this is Mrs. Howe and Mrs. Lindsay sitting in front of you."

That was all he needed. From then on his profane insults had a personal touch, aimed at Gordie and Ted. I took it as long as I could, then I stood up, leaned over two rows, and smacked him smartly with my program. His glasses fell off. The ushers swooped down and hauled him away. Later, after sobering up, he apologized. So did I.

During the 1974 season, the trainer for the new San Diego team came up to me before a game and said, "Mrs. Howe, you don't remember me, but the last time I saw you, you really whacked some guy in Ontario."

I blushed and said I wished he didn't have such a good memory. I normally think of myself as being a controlled and reasonable person. I know how to grit my teeth, though anyone reading these incidents, which covered many years but are now compressed in a few pages, may get a different impression. But one particular scene in Ontario I prefer to attribute to the strain of long hours on the junior hockey programs and a touch of flu.

At any rate, I tolerated it while this fan a few rows back started in on the Howe brothers, before the first puck was even dropped. I could handle it when he said, "Your old man was never any good, Mark Baby, and you sure take after him."

But then the language turned vulgar, and he began to spray his remarks around to the rest of the family, including Cathy and Murray. I suppose those less endowed with common sense just get their thrills by abusing strangers.

The attempts of well-meaning people in the adjoining seats to quiet him failed. I don't know what made me do it. But I calmly excused myself, got out of my seat, walked up the aisle, expressionless, took my program, and cracked him across the ear.

"I am sick of listening to you," I said. "Don't you say one more ugly word about the Howe family."

He was stunned. "Who are you, lady?"

Still threatening him with my raised and tattered program, I said, "One more word about the Howe family and you'll find out who I am."

At that, the fans started applauding. Below us the entire Detroit Junior Wing team turned around. None of them knew what had happened. Mark and Marty just saw me waving the program wildly and feared the worst. But after the game, their teammates crowded around me and said, "Gee, Mrs. Howe, we want you on *our* team."

I take no pleasure from losing my composure, though I admit there is a certain feeling of redemption. But what *can* you do? Call the Civil Liberties Union? I know of few places outside the sports arena where a performer or his family has to suffer that kind of abuse. At least, you needn't suffer it gladly.

Fans can be the meanest part of hockey. Gordie has had his life threatened at least once. Another player received a call from a fan who told him, falsely and maliciously, that his mother had died. As far as I'm concerned, the price of a ticket entitles the spectator to see the game, cheer for his team, and boo the other side. It does not entitle him to spit on players, use obscene language, or attempt to physically abuse a player or official.

The officials, of course, are a kind of human dart board. They have no home turf. Wherever they go, they are in enemy territory. Officials are human, they make mistakes, and I have fussed at my share. But they are out there with no armor other than their own courage. There is no excuse, ever, for the kind of hate fans often spew upon them.

I suspect that a good deal of the fans' misconduct or false courage comes out of a can or bottle or glass. In Houston, hostesses serve drinks to the VIP section in their seats. A fan half in the bag has been known to stagger onto the ice, or challenge a player or official after a game, an act of lunacy if there ever was one. The players are tired, sore as hell if they have lost, and not prepared to suffer fools gladly. Thank goodness, the majority of fans are not this way.

One way or another, hockey has given us whatever we have. It enabled Gordie and me to provide a better life for our family than he could even imagine as a child. Hockey, for Gordie and so many poor Canadian boys, was a way out of the cellar of the have-nots. It has kept a lot of aimless youngsters out of the streets and alleys and given them an opportunity to channel their aggressions. I used to joke that minor hockey kept the kids off the streets and the parents out of the bars.

It has given our sons a chance to travel and see a world they had known only in books. It taught them about pain. About winning. About losing. About life.

I knew Marty was learning a lesson that would stay with him forever after his Pee Wee team lost what was, to them, an important game. He was ten years old. They were eliminated in an invitational tournament in Quebec, which is the most prestigious tourney for youngsters on the continent. The other kids were in the dressing room, angrily flinging their uniforms and gear on the floor, crying and moping in disappointment. I went in to help them get organized to leave. You would have thought the world had come to an end.

But Marty wasn't crying. Or moping. He was going about his business, occasionally whistling, and methodically stuffing his gear into his bag. I said, "Boy, you sure wouldn't know that Marty Howe had lost a game."

He looked at me squarely. "Mother," he said, "I played the very best game I could play. I couldn't play any better. I don't have anything to cry about." I realized then that I had a very mature son.

His father is the same way. Never ashamed of losing, only of playing less than his best. You have to be able to look the team, and yourself, in the eye and say, I didn't let either of us down. You have to be able to say that you gave it everything you had, and it helps if you have the capacity to forgive and forget.

When we returned to Texas from the Canadian-Russian series in the fall of 1974, a letter was waiting on Gordie's desk—an echo of nearly twenty-five years ago. It was from Conn Smythe, who had been one of the great warlord N.H.L. founders, congratulating him on his play in the series. The letter said, in part, "I know Ted Kennedy would love to hear from you someday, stating to him you didn't blame him for your head injury."

Gordie wrote back to Conn and asked him to pass it on to Ted, that he never felt and never told anyone, that it had been Ted's fault. As far as Gord was concerned it was an accident, and the reaction of the press and some of the Red Wings had bothered him. He finished his letter to Conn, "You can tell Ted, in fact, I think he woke me up."

It was after his recovery from the injury, that Gordie went on to break record after record. And across a span of twenty-five years, an old piece of luggage was quietly put away.

8
Howe Enterprises: Keeping Score

SITTING IN MY SEAT at the Olympia one night before a game, years ago, I found myself eavesdropping unintentionally on two women sitting in front of me. One poked the other and said, "Take a look at those Red Wings' uniforms. I've seen them play on the road and, believe me, Shirley, the uniforms *never* look that good. Whoever does the laundry when they travel, sure doesn't do as good a job as the players' wives when the team is home. My, they just sparkle."

That was my cue, I suppose, to tap her on the shoulder and hold up a giant box of soap suds and tell her about my favorite detergent. It would have made a neat television commercial. But, dammit, you can never find someone from Madison Avenue when you really need them.

Visions of Pat Lindsay or Edna Gadsby or me trying to *outwhite* each other danced in my head, and it was all I could do to keep from laughing out loud. For the benefit of that lady and any others of the same impression, let me assure you that I have never washed one of Gordie Howe's uniforms in my life. I doubt, really, that he would have trusted me with it. I *have* done my share of the family laundry, which always included scrubbing the kids' jerseys, pants, and socks. But in my first twenty-seven years of marriage I did a bit more than stay home and wash dirty socks.

There have been many famous and colorful lines in hockey—the Production Line, the Go-Go-Go Line, the Kraut Line. In recent years we discovered a new one—the Bottom Line. When the three Howes signed a $2 million plus contract with Houston in the summer of 1973, I was suddenly catapulted into running a million-dollar business. That contract called for more dollars than Gordie had been paid during the total of all the years he played with the Detroit Red Wings.

I have always had the reputation of being the godmother of the family, the one who tells a client, "Make me a deal I can't refuse." I had started out, like many wives, doing the elementary chores such as house payments and keeping the insurance updated while Gordie was on the road. At home, I set aside a room as an office to answer fan mail and coordinate his appearances. As Gordie's career grew and we began making investments and the endorsement market picked up for hockey players, I found myself running a nearly full-time office—still out of our home.

It is a fact of life that the security of their aging players, even those who have been *stars,* is not a felt concern in most pro sports organizations. By the end of his career in Detroit, we realized that if Gordie was to enjoy an active and financially rewarding future, we would have to do it ourselves. By 1973 Howe Enterprises was far more complicated than balancing our accounts and paying the light bill.

We set up an office in Houston in a building partly owned by Irvin Kaplan, the majority owner of the Aeros. Irvin and his wife, Molly Ann, had gone to some lengths to make our relocation as painless as possible. In fact, they even helped us select our home.

Dorothy Ringler, who had been Gordie's secretary in Detroit, decided also to pull up stakes. She and her husband, Rocky, a retired Detroit policeman, followed us to Texas. Dorothy and I work a forty-hour week taking care of business matters for the three Howe hockey players. Most of our contacts are with Detroit, Canada, and eastern associates, so we operate the office on an Eastern Standard Time schedule: eight A.M. to four P.M., Houston time.

After that publicized package-contract with the Aeros had been signed, we were suddenly faced with the delightful problem of more responsibility and more dollars and what to do with them. I felt a pressure I couldn't identify and still can't, because all at once I was talking in numbers my brain had never before tried to absorb. That's quite an impact. How to use the money wisely is the key factor. Not so much for us. Gordie's comeback was a sort of epilogue to a long career. But the boys were just starting out; given their potential, it was important to make the most of it from the beginning.

We had reason to believe—to hope—that they would have long and successful careers in hockey and enjoy all the fringe rewards that now went with it. But you can't *plan* on it. Careers can end in an eye blink. You had to make the most of the money already in the till. And to add as many safeguards as possible.

Sports has become in this country a rich new force, due to the times and a number of odd circumstances that came together at once. Few athletes ever expected to accumulate wealth directly from their actions in the arena. If this was accomplished at all, it was through business contacts that were the spoils of fame and the romance of sport.

But the influx of television money into football, the expansion of pro sports from border to border, and the arrival of competing new leagues raised the pay scale for athletes to levels that once would have bought an entire franchise. The

Howes, among others, are indeed wealthy men today simply as a result of the salaries their sports have paid them.

I questioned if our finances had grown too big for me to handle. Perhaps the time had arrived to call in professional help. Managing an athlete's money has turned out to be big business. Gordie never had an exclusive agent and, for most of his career, never needed one. At one time we contacted Mark McCormack, the first of the super agents, who represented Arnold Palmer among others.

"I'm just not interested," he told Gordie, "in handling hockey players."

Now McCormack was calling us. And Gordie was still smarting from what he considered a slap in the face of his profession. "I was big then," he said. "Why am I suddenly so different now?"

I suggested to Gord that perhaps we should forget about past slights and think seriously about signing with the McCormack group. This *was* the one area in which Howe Enterprises lacked muscle. We had an excellent attorney, accountant, and insurance man. I could manage our finances as before, but I didn't have the time to make trips to New York to seek out the key people and push for the big endorsement contracts. From our discussions, we soon learned that Mark McCormack insisted on his office controlling practically everything if he took you on as a client. It would be, in that zippy Madison Avenue idiom, a "total marriage." They were very professional, the kind of outfit we really needed. But the decision to turn everything over to them was a heavy one—too heavy, as it turned out.

I had my own mixed emotions about whether to wipe my hands clean entirely and unburden myself of the marketing and endorsements for the Howes. I had so many roles to play. I wanted to be home to prepare the game meals. I wanted to be free to take part in Cathy's activities. I wanted to work with

Houston's youth-hockey programs, and continue to give my time to the March of Dimes and other charities. However, I wasn't kidding myself. I knew I couldn't pretend to think I could do the job these people could do for our family.

We had a family summit meeting to discuss the matter. Finally, Mark spoke up. "Mother," he said, "even if we receive less than we would otherwise, I have faith in what you can do. I want you to work with these things. Let's keep it in the family."

So Howe Enterprises remained a Ma and Pa operation. After I recovered from the initial shock of handling not one but three well-paid professional athletes, things started running smoothly. I made the promotional commitments for them, negotiated the contracts, kept them up to date on their cash-flow sheets and investments, made sure they had proper insurance coverage. I also handled the fan and business mail, and made recommendations on investing their money based largely on research and professional advice. And once in a while I picked up their dry cleaning. As far as the last item is concerned, I sometimes get taken advantage of, and have to put my foot down.

I keep a huge calendar on which I juggle our Houdini act. From Cathy's social dates to Gordie's golf dates, from dental appointments to conferences with attorneys, from appearances to interviews—it all goes down on the master sheet. Even our weekly calls to Murray are penciled in—not that anyone needs to remind me when it's time to talk to my youngest and see how his game is going. The family always joked, "If the house ever burns down, grab Mom's calendar first."

My business experience came not from having any important positions with large firms but literally from home. There I drafted letters for Gordie's fan mail and filled the requests for autographed pictures. Every mail delivery was a grab bag. Some people wrote to ask for skates or sticks. Others requested a get-well note for a friend in the hospital. School children wanted bios and pictures, and parents wanted Gordie to tell their kids to eat their vegetables and go to school. I sorted them all and took care of those I felt deserved a reply.

We considered the fans, Joe Public, the most important of all the people to whom we had an obligation. If they didn't like us, didn't buy tickets, we were out of a job. In my opinion, answering the mail was essential. Any time our kids wrote anyone, I was terribly disappointed for them if they didn't receive a reply.

Many fans invited us to their weddings and bar mitzvahs. Of course, we couldn't go, but I always saw to it that Gordie had an appropriate letter of good wishes to put in the return mail. There were regular mailings from dedicated pen pals who sent us poems, cards on birthdays and anniversaries, their favorite receipes, and just lovely thoughts. Once in a while a letter would appear that made you sit down and think about yourself and your life.

Once, Gordie received a letter from a judge explaining that he was trying a case in Detroit involving a youngster named Gordie Howe. The judge had told the boy, "Don't you know whose name you have? Don't you think Gordie would be disappointed in what has been happening with your life?"

The judge asked Gordie if he would write a few lines to his namesake. We spent a lot of time drafting that letter. We wanted to inspire that boy, if we could, to be aware and useful and spend his hours as the irreplaceable gems they are. So we told him about Gord's childhood, what it meant to work and to improve, to have pride, and to learn to like yourself. We mailed the letter, addressing it in care of the judge, who gave it to the boy and placed him on probation. We lost track of the boy after that, and I suspect that is a good sign. I have a feeling he turned out all right.

Sometimes, when I read of rare autographs going for huge prices at a gallery, I smile and think of Gord. If there is a market for his autographs years from now they will go for pennies because he must have signed so many thousands. Whenever he had to attend an event where he would be expected to give out autographs, I would bring home a few hundred or so photos each night so he could sign them. He would spend hours doing it, so no one would receive a stamped autograph.

Inevitably, some fan would complain, "Don't give *me* one of those stamped jobs. I want you to sign mine, that's the least you could do."

Gordie, never learning, would try to convince her that he had actually signed all those autographs, that the signatures were really his. Needless to say, it was a lost cause.

I made it a point to answer some of the critical mail myself. Some I toss in the waste basket. When someone denounced Gordie, for whatever reason, I often would write back with passion, pointing out how hard he worked for the team and how much of his free time he devoted to charity.

One woman wrote back to Gordie and said, "Your wife is nothing but a professional letter writer." She was determined to have the last say.

Gordie's easy disposition once caused him some embarrassment. We had gone to visit a Dr. Ronayne, whose youngsters were in the same hockey program as ours. As soon as the kids in the neighborhood discovered Gordie was there, they all showed up at the back door for autographs. Like most doctors, this one had a number of note pads which pharmacies distribute to medical offices. Not glancing at the other side, Gord started freely signing his name on the back of these pages—with appropriate comments, such as good luck, best wishes.

It didn't take long for the calls to start coming in from giggling parents. On the other side of the autographs Gordie had signed were douche instructions for women. We all had a few hysterics over that, and I jokingly advised our doctor friend to be more discriminating about the scratch pads he left around his home. I also chided Gordie that this was what happened when he didn't let me manage his publicity.

In those early years we had no big money to invest. My main duties were running the house and handling the bills and day-to-day finances. Unlike football players, the hockey types were not in demand for endorsements. You were lucky to get a speaking date for twenty-five dollars. But it actually was from those household business experiences that I later learned how to handle substantial sums of money. And, to coin a phrase, any woman can.

We bought our first home in 1953, and it represented our first major investment. We felt from the beginning that it was unwise to put our money in someone else's pocket. Instead of seeing it go down the drain in rent, we wanted to build up an equity. We have always owned a home. Gordie wasn't yet making substantial money, nor did we have any major cash reserves. He had kept his promise to himself to buy a house for his parents, a gesture he never regretted. But as the family and the income increased, we moved into bigger homes, adding a bedroom or garage along the way.

I started out by doing a lot of leg work for Gord, the kinds of things he couldn't do while he was on the road. When we were looking for a house I would scout the market, narrow the choices down to four or five homes, and wait for Gord. We'd make the decision together.

With a husband who traveled for weeks at a time, I learned to cope with a number of things out of sheer necessity. If emergency plumbing needed to be done, I really couldn't wait until Gordie got home. Little by little, I was gaining experience in contracting work to be done and looking out for whatever interests we had.

At heart, Gordie wanted to be involved only in his hockey. He disliked all the other preliminaries, finding and dealing with insurance people and attorneys and contracts and investments. My job, I felt, was to relieve him of the financial pressures and decisions so he could devote his time and concern to the game. Meanwhile, I found myself more and more engulfed in these matters.

Not that I didn't get stung along the way. Like everyone else, we had our shaggy-dog stories and our heart-rending, Better Business Bureau dramas. Two of the biggest stings happened on purely household matters. All of us loved animals and were in the service of several along the way. Our luck wasn't always good when it came to canines.

We once were given a German shepherd pup we had no time to train. Each day I'd go out to the garage to cart the boys off to one of their games, and I'd find that he had decorated the entire garage floor. I'd have to go into action with my super-duper-pooper-scooper while the kids sat in the car laughing their heads off. This dog was definitely not adding to the Howe family harmony. Eventually, we gave him to a blind friend, Jim Sebes.

Much later we decided to buy a full-grown, well-trained shepherd that would not only be a pet but would offer protection as well. We found just the dog we wanted and bought him from an ex-policeman. We no sooner had gotten him and learned to love him when he ran away. The kids were in tears. I was in tears. We placed an ad in the local paper, and the next day a man called and asked if we were the ones who had advertised the lost dog, and he described him.

I was so grateful, I said, "Oh, yes, yes, that's him. Do come over, and we'll gladly give you a reward."

He exploded. "Madam," he said, "I would like to know what makes you think this is your dog. This happens to be *our* dog and he disappeared a week ago. I'd like to know how you acquired him. You have a lot of nerve stealing someone else's pet."

I couldn't believe what he was saying. But I knew something strange was going on. I suggested he come over and talk to us. Gordie and I visited with him, and the three of us finally figured out that the dog had been stolen from him and sold to the unsuspecting, gullible Howes. We decided it was time to give the ex-cop, whose credibility we had never questioned, a call.

Under the pretense that we had found the dog but something was wrong with it, we asked him to drop by. When he walked in and saw us with the dog's owner who, it turned out, lived near him, his face fell like a window shade. He refunded our money for the "hot dog" and left, but we were still the losers, having grown attached to a pet that wasn't ours.

I learned another lesson the hard way. While the kids were growing up, Gordie and I realized we had too many things going. Do-it-yourselfers or not, we needed some help. I noticed our neighbors had some landscapers who seemed to be doing a great job on their property. I hired them to take care of our lawn and yard, knowing that Gordie and I would be gone much of the summer. I then proceeded to make one of my first business mistakes. I thought I could encourage them to do a better job by paying them in advance. So they wouldn't have to bother billing us each month, I paid them for the *entire* summer.

They showed up the first week and never came back. I was not just furious, I was volcanic. I told Gordie, when we got home that fall and saw what a mess our lawn and shrubs were, "If I ever catch up with those guys, they are going to refund every penny." They weren't showing up at the neighbors', either, for obvious reasons. But the neighbors didn't suffer any loss. They hadn't paid in advance.

About six months later, Gordie and I went bowling with

friends from our summer league. We had just finished and were walking out of the place when, by chance, I happened to spot one of the landscaping men.

I clutched Gordie by the elbow and hissed, "Do you see what I see?" He didn't know what I was talking about, not having dealt with them himself. I said, "That's one of the landscapers who gave us the royal rip-off."

I kept an eye on him for the next several minutes. He was putting on a show for his friends, talking and laughing loudly.

Gordie tried to pacify me. "Now, be careful" he said, "don't do or say something you'll regret."

But I couldn't contain myself. I thought, if this guy had enough nerve to pull what he did, I had enough nerve to chew him out in front of his friends.

With that I walked right out on the alley where he was hefting his bowling ball. I tapped him on the shoulder and said, "Do you remember me?" He stood there dumbfounded while I tore into him. "You know," I concluded, "you are just despicable. You and your crew really had a lot of nerve, taking our money, then never showing up all summer."

Gordie was standing in the back, laughing, because this was my feisty side taking charge. On our way out he said, "You know, you're something else." But he enjoyed every minute of it. Especially the look on the fellow's face.

We never went after the fellow legally; it wasn't worth it. But I learned an important business principal: *Never* pay for services up front.

As Gordie's income increased we started to seek out investments. We wanted security. We had no idea he would end up playing twenty-five seasons with Detroit, and during the last fifteen of those years we were still saying we needed to find something for the future.

Our first attempts all cratered. Gord and Al Kaline, Ted Lindsay, Frank Carlin, and Marty Pavelich formed a business called Mapko Engineering. We had hoped this business, an auto tool-design company, would become a kind of life net into which Gordie could leap if he was injured or retired. This was the business whose profits Jack Adams feared would ruin the boys. It never generated any income and eventually folded.

Gordie, Frank, and Kaline, the popular hitting star of the baseball Tigers, then started a manufacturers' rep company. None of them could give much time to it and this enterprise also went down the drain eventually. Out of numerous requests, we attempted to franchise hockey schools across the country, but many of the people we sold franchises to didn't measure up, and we were forced to dissolve them. Finally, a company called Gordie Howe Business Forms also fizzled. Lack of time, and often knowledge, led to these failures. But we took the position, nothing ventured, nothing gained.

This sort of sputtering business start is not uncommon for professional athletes, who are as susceptible to easy ideas that promise instant riches as anyone, if not more so. By the nature of their jobs, the isolation of their skills, they are conditioned to leave the nuts and bolts to others. Misled by the cheers and press clippings and the frenzied exposure of sports, they confuse image with success. At one time, in the space of a few weeks, I remember reading that half a dozen pro athletes had declared bankruptcy as a result of unwise business ventures, among them Jerry Lucas (basketball), Denny McLain (baseball), and Lance Alworth (football).

Most of the ideas that attracted Gordie were regarded as immediate security. Everyone was ready to jump in, but no master plan was created and what first appeared to be a substantial concept soon proved valueless. Gordie didn't have the time to run things himself. We needed to look for investments that were managed by competent people.

In the 1950s the endorsement market wasn't that big in pro sports and simply didn't exist for hockey players. Joe Namath opened it up for everyone in the late sixties, appearing on the tube peddling shave cream, electric razors, airlines, popcorn poppers, and finally making the ultimate score, stretching across the screen in a pair of pantyhose.

But Gordie Howe landed what was the first long-term advertising contract any hockey player had ever signed. In 1964 he agreed to a ten-year contract with the T. Eaton department store chain in Canada for $10,000 a year. That doesn't sound like much in today's market, but it was a bonanza then and Gordie and I worked out the contract with an attorney friend, Marv Larivee.

Slowly, but surely, other endorsements began to come our way even though we lacked the contacts professional agents enjoyed. Some athletes get so wrapped up in the fringe business that they lose sight of what got them there—the sport itself. Hockey always came first with Gordie. He would never ask a coach to excuse him from a practice session to make a television filming or a personal appearance. He passed up a few dollars, but he can look in his mirror and tell himself he never did anything to jeopardize his team. That always meant something to him, however cornball it may sound to the cynics.

It was only from about 1967 that we finally had accumulated enough capital to make some major investments. At that time I went through the tribulations of finding good attorneys and good accountants. We experienced several disappointments along the way, at one point paying through the nose for very little legal advice. You learn as you grow, just as we did in the business ventures. In time, fortunately, the pluses began to outweigh the minuses, and we soon started to think in terms of diversifying. That's Wall Street jargon for not letting yourself get wiped out in one bad deal. You spread the risk.

When Gordie retired the first time, we tried to expand even more. He continued to operate out of his office at the

Olympia, and I worked at home, where we kept all of our personal files and papers. In 1972 we started investing with John Curran, a friend of ours, in apartment complexes. Whenever John went into an investment, he offered a piece of it to Gord. With him, we also got involved with the seed-stock breeding of Polled Hereford cattle in Michigan, a real love for us because of our fondness for animals. We even bought stock in the Calderone Curran ranch, managed by John's partner, Tony Calderone.

Just before Gordie and the boys signed with the Aeros, we established a corporation called Progressive Goals, Inc., which owns Gordie Howe Agri Labs, a distributor for a product called Silo-Guard. It controls the fermentation of silage fed to cattle. If the Aeros contract hadn't come along, Gordie would have become more active with Silo-Guard and his other interests and dropped out of hockey. In the two years since he had retired as a player, our estate had almost doubled.

But the Aeros did happen, and suddenly I found myself handling twelve sets of books and trying to manage the financial lives of three hockey players. Here the boys were, drawing more in interest alone on their savings than Gordie made in his season in the minors at Omaha—$2,300. And counting bonuses, they were both making more than Gordie had earned in his last season in Detroit.

We started talking and negotiating in terms of package deals involving all three. At first, the requests kept coming in for Gordie alone. He had the name and the record and the credibility. I worked hard at convincing companies that the boys would appeal to the youth market. The demand for them came, but it came slowly. Endorsements, after all, had only produced serious money for Gordie in the last five years.

It is a pleasant way to earn a living, but I don't mean to sound consumed by it. A Texas oil millionaire was once asked why he continued to work, to deal, to spend hard days making more money than he could possibly live long enough to spend.

"After a certain point," he said, "the money isn't why you do it. It has no meaning. It is just a way of keeping score."

There are many ways, but that isn't a bad one.

We have tried hard not to chase a buck. We didn't go knocking on doors. But when people came to us, we followed the rules for negotiating I had established earlier. They had worked well for us in long-term contracts that had been set up with, among others, Lincoln Mercury, whose sports panel included Jesse Owens, Al Kaline, Byron Nelson, and Tony Trabert. Gordie was pleased, not just with the money and the two cars they provided us, but with the chance it gave him to rub shoulders with other athletes he respected. Gordie had also represented the Bank of Nova Scotia and, more recently, joined the Sears panel of advisors.

Endorsements usually start with a phone call. If the proposal has any interest for us at all, I suggest that it be put in writing. This usually separates the men from the boys, and there can be no misunderstanding between the other party and myself. I review it, get some legal advice, check to see if there are any conflicts with the league, and then ask our accountant to see how the program fits in terms of dollars.

If the proposal figure is low, I make a counter offer, which is step two. If the company involved accepts, we move to step three, which is to draw the final agreement. Our attorney drafts that, although for smaller projects I may draw the letter of intent myself. Gordie and/or the boys sign the contract. In step four I begin to coordinate whatever new obligations are created with the rest of his schedule.

At times someone will call who's not quite sure what an appropriate figure would be. I simply quote the famous line from the movie, *The Godfather*, and say, "Make me an offer I can't refuse." That usually breaks the ice, and we go on from there. I consider myself a hard-nosed businesswoman, meaning that once a price is established it doesn't fluctuate. That would hardly be fair to the companies who have already paid it.

Of course, sometimes you quote a figure that's intentionally high to discourage an offer you know Gordie doesn't want—say, a one-day appearance halfway across the country. I did that once, throwing out a figure I considered outrageous, and to my surprise the caller said, "Fine, we'll look forward to having him." Most of them, however, just gulp and say they'll get back to you.

If a flat fee is involved and we know the people, we usually bill them later. Gordie and the boys will not accept cash payments. Too often that smacks of a way of dodging taxes, and we prefer to keep a clean slate.

The Howes don't charge for charity appearances. Many athletes do, figuring that if a man attends a banquet that raises $30,000 or more, the budget ought to be able to afford a $1,000 fee for the speaker. In some cases Gordie will ask for expenses, but he won't accept a fee. We have worked with the 4-H Foundation, the March of Dimes, the Arthritis Foundation, and others, and we do it because that, too, is a way of keeping score. It is time we enjoy giving.

I am probably not the easiest of people to get along with in business. I expect a great deal. Our Houston attorney, Harrison Vickers, and Bob Weinstein our Minnesota lawyer, are the kind of well-ordered individuals I prefer. If they tell you they are going to call at three, you can set your watch by the ring of the phone. I'm a strong believer in protecting yourself at the front, so you don't have to protect yourself in the end.

Contracts aren't the only way to accomplish this. By the time we are ready to put our names on the line, we have gotten to know the people well enough to know if they are substantive. Are they first class, credible, reliable? I dislike intensely the idea of having to worry about someone else failing to come through after we have done our part or of having to wave a contract over their heads, threatening to sue to get the job done. If we are going to have that kind of hassle, I want no part of it.

I am a stickler, almost a fanatic, for detail. If someone doesn't follow through with me the first time around, it's unlikely there will be a second chance. I used to give the benefit of the doubt, but I don't have time now. The load is too heavy. I find myself unable to afford the luxury of being tolerant of laziness or incompetence. I don't want to be jockeyed around. This attitude is made clear ahead of time to the people with whom we associate. I don't think I'm hard to please. It's just that I dislike being told someone will follow through and then find I'm left holding the bag.

Much of my time during the first months in Houston were spent setting up banking, estate, and investment programs for the boys. For one thing—and this may sound strange in view of their ages—they needed wills. These were drawn for them, and until the time Marty and Mark have families of their own, our younger children will be their beneficiaries.

The first endorsement the boys landed was for the Munro air hockey game called "The Howe Hockey Game." That, I think, was a natural. We tried to key in on some avenues in which the boys could begin to save part of their money, and invest some. They purchased interests in two apartment complexes, they own some purebred cattle, and hold stock in two banks.

I keep Marty and Mark informed about all transactions. Very often I tape meetings to be played back when they have time to listen. I want them to learn how to take care of their own finances. I keep regular cash-flow sheets so they'll know where their money is going. We have introduced them to bank borrowing. Gordie and I learned early how important it is to establish credit and to keep a good rating.

Our bank accounts and our financial statements have changed dramatically since we hit the sweepstakes in Houston. But I honestly don't think our life-styles have changed that much. The boys particularly have been asked a thousand times, "Now that you're a pro and earning big money for your age, how has it changed you?" The answer is, not much. Marty has a car, and he was as excited as anyone else when he finally made his last monthly payment.

Mark, who spent his first year in Houston without wheels, bought a van. It's lake blue, the Aeros' color. This was his first big purchase, and he was ecstatic. Both boys now have a few more clothes in their closets, not because they suddenly turned into peacocks but because of all the traveling in which they are involved. Mark bought a stereo—not exactly unheard of for young man going on nineteen.

Basically, they live like other young men. There have been no major alterations. Yes, they have money, but most of it they don't see. It's all on paper, and I don't think they are constantly aware of how much they have. They ask questions. They want to know what is happening, and they want to be in on the decisions. But it's not as if the greenbacks were dangling from every light fixture. I haven't noticed either of them turning into playboy types.

As for the family fortress, we live in a home that "sprawls" more than the others we have owned. There's a swimming pool in the back yard. In addition, there's a putting green with a city street sign, "Howe Corner," watching over the terrain. I was able to buy the new furniture we needed all at once, instead of one piece at a time, as I did during most of our marriage. There are a few more clothes in my own closet, and it's a walk-in. We live an affluent life but not an extravagant one. You are more likely to see us eating pizza and salad in the kitchen than making the scene in Houston's plush restaurants. The times we do dine out, we choke on the bill just like anyone else.

Gordie basically is the same person I met back at the Lucky Strike, amid the music of crashing pins. His thinking about people and what makes him happy and relaxed—these things remain the same.

What has changed is our pace. Our careers, new earnings, and investments make us work harder—to improve ourselves, I hope, not just to put money in the bank. My pace, in particular, has quickened. The phone rings almost daily with endorsement offers or deals or salesmen. One guy called about a T-shirt giveaway program he wanted to tie in with a food chain. A brokerage firm in Canada called, wanting an endorsement from Gordie. My counter suggestion was a Howe package.

"You know," I said, "with the stock market the way it is, it wouldn't hurt to have a couple of young faces promoting some younger investors for you."

The one market we haven't really penetrated is the television-commerical industry. Gordie did do one, as a favor to the league, for the Phoenix Roadrunners, which was eventually sold to other teams. The film showed Gordie standing on the ice as an off-camera voice said: "Gordie Howe, hockey's leading scorer—twenty-six years a pro, twenty-two times an All Star." Gordie skates up and stops. The camera zooms in. While the announcer talks, he is tossing a puck in the air. The voice asks, "Gordie, what do you think of the Phoenix Roadrunners this year?" For a split second they cut away to an action clip on the ice, then back to Gordie. They've switched the puck for a chocolate cupcake. Gord looks straight into the camera, doesn't crack a smile, just squeezes the puck, which crumbles in his hand.

I keep dreaming up wacky commercial ideas for the three

Howes. One would be for the shampoo product that "gets the gray out of your hair." Marty and Mark are outside the Coliseum, signing autographs, surrounded by pretty girls. Then out comes Gordie, who has just shampooed the gray right out of his hair. The girls drop the boys and rush over to Gord. As they walk away into the city lights, Mark turns to Marty and says, "Gee, we'd better tell Mom to hide the hair stuff from Dad."

Fade. Cut. And print.

At times I still wonder if Howe Enterprises hasn't outgrown us. Perhaps we will need to call in more professionals. Late in 1974 we hired a bookkeeper, Mary Ann Staha, our first Texas employee. But I cling to the idea of running it as a family operation. I would love some day to see Cathy, who is developing into a bright and pretty young lady, involved in the company. She has already worked summers doing the fan mail and learning part of the routine. She works well with people.

While I don't identify myself with the women's liberation movement, I guess I do have some liberated ideas. Gordie respects my business instincts and my ability to run things. But I have been in a unique position. If Cathy was sick, there was no way I was going to be at the office. As my own boss, I could walk out the door and be home where I felt I was needed.

We even keep a business telephone and office at the house, so if I need to be home, if someone is sick, or I'm waiting for the roofer, I can keep in touch with my work. When Gordie is in town, the office is technically his. He may be there in the morning, and I'll work in the afternoon. He kids me and says, "Is it okay if I sit in your chair?"

When we're both there we'll ignore the desk and pull up chairs around the conference table.

Actually, I have two full-time jobs—one at home, the other at Howe enterprises. When the kids lean on me too hard I don't hesitate to tell them to pick up their own dry cleaning and cash their own checks. Through the years I have found it important that I don't shortchange *me*.

But from the beginning I've worn many hats and thrived on it. I have never believed that a woman is *just* a housewife or *just* a mother. I consider her role the most important factor leading to family stability. Women should take special pride in what they do for their families. Of all the roles I have played through the years, there is one I like best—being Gordie Howe's lover. I like doing a good job at that, too.

9
From Russia,
Without Love

THE TRADITIONS OF SPORT, even professional sport, are so strong that they constitute a set of *rules* involving fellowship, fair play, courtesy, a sense of common ground.

I reminded myself of this in hopes of shaking the uneasiness most of us shared as our Air Canada charter, out of Helsinki, began its descent into Moscow. We were bound for the final leg of the Team-Canada Russian series in October 1974. I hesitate to use the word *foreboding*, lest this begin to sound like a sequel to *The Kremlin Letter*. But we were nervous, excited, wary, and nothing we had heard up to then had done much to reassure us.

Those players who had been there during the 1972 matches had warned us that the landing would not be routine. I mean, this wasn't Honolulu, where girls in grass skirts welcome you with colorful leis and alluring gestures.

"Before you land," we had been told, "the pilot will be advised that he is under the control of the USSR. And when the plane pulls up, soldiers with guns will be there to meet you."

I got goose bumps when the pilot flipped on the intercom and told us to fasten our seat belts because we were approaching Moscow. He added—no reason for alarm, he said—that the approach and guide controls were quite foreign to the Canadian crew. While he expected nothing *untoward*, he wanted us to be aware that he might have to divert at the last moment.

Years earlier, with great effort, I had conquered a rather entrenched fear of flying. I was one of those people whose knuckles turn white from gripping the armrests and who, at the slightest noise, look to see if a wing has fallen off. Now, high over Mother Russia, I had to fight down the panic I thought I had long since left behind me.

From the moment the wheels hit the runway in Moscow, there began what I now see in retrospect as a calculated game of one-upmanship. It was a crude effort to unsettle us, a taffy pull to see whether we or they controlled our emotions. I suspect the Russians won.

Like school children learning the tactics of fire drills, we had been briefed again and again by the people from the travel bureau and by the team's general manager, Bill Hunter, as to exactly how we would deplane—how we would handle our visas, the customs declarations, the luggage.

We had been assured that our official party would be whisked through customs as quickly as the Russians had when they arrived for the games held earlier in Montreal. Detente was supposed to be alive and well at the customs and baggage checkpoints. The press was to deplane first. We knew the Russians had their sights set on hosting the 1980 Olympics, and they were anxious, we felt sure, to show the world a side not generally reported, a country of charm and elegance and dignity. After the writers, the players, and their wives and families had deplaned, the team officials, the steering committee, friends, and owners would follow.

While I was mentally quizzing myself to make sure I had memorized the instructions, I could see through my window the soldiers and trucks pulling up to the plane. The door opened, and up the ramp came our first greeter. He informed Billy Hunter that the original procedure was no longer in effect. Only the press and the players would get off, which we assumed was a Russian courtesy to speed the team on its way to a scheduled practice. But being separated from their families so abruptly gave the players and the rest of us a moment of dismay. We knew that once the team was on the ground, if the Russians for whatever reason decided to tell the pilot to take off, the plane *would* take off.

We had no choice but to do as we were told. The players left, glancing nervously over their shoulders, while we waited, cramped in our seats, for another half hour. Finally, we were allowed to leave the plane. They herded us like cattle onto a bus built to hold half as many, and we struggled to hang on to our hand baggage as we rattled on to the terminal. There the fun began. Wives were to go through one channel. Owners another. Mothers with children another. They had a bin and a category for everyone.

A half hour was consumed in checking our passports before we were cleared to proceed to the luggage area. And there, twiddling their thumbs, were the players we thought had been whisked off to practice two hours ago. Instead, they were still waiting for their bags—twenty-seven weary, frustrated, neglected characters who were half the reason for anyone being anywhere. By that time, of course, any thought of practice had been scrubbed.

They were like the legendary mouse who no longer wanted the cheese—he just wanted to get his tail out of the trap.

Eventually, without the aid of bellhops or skycaps, we wrestled our own luggage onto the bus—all of us, that is, except for six players whose luggage had not yet been found, even though all of it came on the same plane, which had made no stops. The Howes batted a thousand. Gordie, Mark, and

Marty were among the six whose luggage was mysteriously missing. They stayed behind to wait for the bags.

By the time I left the airport it was dark. I could see little on the bus ride into Moscow except vague images of homes and buildings. As we reached the heart of the city, I could see the broad boulevards, the Gothic buildings, and hundreds of people walking the streets. It was October, with milder temperatures than one would expect in Russia. Your overwhelming first impression of Moscow is all gray and black, broken only by the golden domes of the Kremlin and the multicolored, onion-topped turrets of historic St. Basil's Cathedral.

We checked into the Russia Hotel, an enormous place with 3,000 rooms. I never did figure out the lobby floor-plan, which was so complicated I called it The Maze. There were four sides to the hotel and a set of eight glass doors at each. It was always a challenge to guess which door would open and where it led. I decided it was designed to keep out the mean winter weather or else the maze gave someone an opportunity to survey who came in and out of the hotel.

I was not allowed to register until Gordie arrived—another hour's wait. Had I known what the rooms looked like, I would have been in no rush at all. By this time the whole gang was tired, cranky, and peeved at the Russian unwelcome. The registration desk was so disorganized it reminded me of a fire sale. The people from our travel bureau, it turned out, had never been to Russia either. It was really the blind leading the sightless.

All of the Howes except Cathy were quartered on the third floor of the hotel. She was on the ninth—a circumstance that concerned me but over which I had no control. Gordie and I were given a room next door to the team physician, Dr. Gerry Wilson. Marty and Mark were down the hall.

We all reached our rooms at about the same time and

discovered there was only one way to get in. You showed your registration to the "key lady" who sat at the end of the hall. You received only one key, no matter how many people were staying in the room. Whenever you left, you returned the key to her. The only time you retained the key to your room was while you were in it.

Turning our precious, united key in the lock, Gordie opened the door to our room. We both froze in our tracks. It was not to be believed. It looked like a flophouse, about ten feet by eleven, so small that if one of us wanted to pace the other had to step out into the hall. It was easy to see how they had managed to divide the place into 3,000 rooms. They were just large closets. There was no television or radio, two items we hadn't really expected and could hardly have used. No stationery. No clock. No postcards. The walls were bare except for one landscaped picture that seemed to have been painted by numbers.

We had not expected a king-sized bed, and they didn't surprise us in this respect. There sat two dinky twin beds slightly wider than a park bench, with sheets like flour sacking. Two high-backed chairs and wobbly table, vintage 1940, a suitcase shelf, and four coat hangers completed the room.

I was convinced. *Dr. Zhivago had died for our sins.*

The beds were clean though we discovered they were not conducive to lovemaking. Or even sleep. The floor looked as if it had never been swept, and emanating from the bathroom was a smell—no, that's not right—emanating from the bathroom was a stench. It took a trip to Russia for me to discover the wonders of American technology, such as gooseneck plumbing. In Russia, the pipes go straight down, and—believe me—the smell can drift right back up again.

I have never considered myself a difficult person to satisfy in matters of comfort. I didn't grow up accustomed to luxury. But I found it hard to believe that this was the hospitality the

Russians intended to offer us. Gordie was about the closest thing to a Canadian hero in Russia. The Russian team had been given the red carpet treatment in Canada. And yet they had bullied us on our arrival, and given us rooms that compared unfavorably to a five-dollar-a-night skid row flophouse.

Most of us were so exhausted and shocked at that point, we were punchy. One by one we came bouncing out of our rooms into the halls, laughing. Dr. Wilson had found cockroaches running around in circles in his bath. He said one was large enough to be a pet. He wished he had time to train it, so he could take it home, design a small leash, and have his nurse tell callers he was out walking his pet cockroach.

Later that night in the dining room we compared stories. We speculated on what a great place this would be to spend a honeymoon. We joked about ordering breakfast via room service, a thought that simply curdled our stomachs.

One gag did come true. Someone had cracked that whoever won the Most Valuable Player Award for the series would probably receive as his prize a week's trip to Moscow, all expenses paid. The guy who came in second would have to stay two weeks.

As it happened, Bobby Hull was named the M.V.P., and his reward *was* a week's vacation in Moscow. We began to wonder if the walls did have ears.

We sat down hopefully to the Canadian steaks that had been flown over for us, but the Russians, alas, didn't know how to cook them. Hockey players have never been famed for their gourmet tastes, and ketchup is one of their standard items of equipment. Never was it so desperately needed. But for reasons possibly known only to the KGB, the cases of ketchup flown in from Canada were impounded for three days.

The Russians are punctual people. We learned that if we

were scheduled to eat from 9 P.M. to 10 P.M., and we were not there by the stroke of nine, we were out of luck. With sixty of us in the dining room, they threw the food at us, and if we weren't finished by ten they had a subtle way of announcing it was time to go. They turned out the lights and the waiters went home.

The Howes, as much as or more than the others, had looked forward to this trip. It wasn't just another junket abroad. It was a unique honor for a father-and-sons combination to play for Team Canada. And Mark, as far as anyone knew, was the first player in the history of international hockey to represent two countries. He had played for the American Olympic team in Japan and brought home a silver medal. Now, because of a ruling that established a dual citizenship for the boys, Mark was representing Team Canada. Ironically, it was Billy Harris, who coached the Canadian team in the Olympics, who was now the coach for Team Canada. For them and for me this was another milestone.

Cathy and I had joined the men in Vancouver where they were finishing the Canadian half of the series. There we had a gay, lighthearted time renewing old hockey acquaintances and getting to know some of the new players. The spirit in the Vancouver press was refreshing. They headlined the series, "Howe in the Hull Can We Lose?"—referring, of course, to the Howes and Bobby Hull, for one of the rare times playing on the same side.

I picked up the phone in our Vancouver hotel room one afternoon and a sweet, overzealous young female voice said breathlessly, "Is this Bobby Hull's room?"

"No," I said, "but if you want Gordie Howe you can have him. But you'll have to go through me." She hung up, apparently unamused.

At the arena that night I sat with Joanne Hull. Playing in spite of an inflamed shoulder, Gordie scored the game's first goal, and I lifted her about three feet off the ground. The rest of the evening she was hoisting me, as Bobby turned the hat trick. Both of the old-timers, Bobby and Gordie, scooped up pucks like they were kids scoring their first goals. Just the same, the Russians ended up tying the game.

At the banquet later, Gordie won the award for being the outstanding player of the game.

"I wonder," he said, when he accepted it, "what Hull has to do to win this thing."

Bobby had pulled the hat trick, but he had received the trophy the night before, and I guess the Russians were spreading the honors around. That sort of grade school morality runs deep in sports, and never fails to surprise me.

Gordie cracked up the crowd by concluding, "I must have beat him by a hair."

The reference was to Hull's new hairpiece. It's simple humor but jocks love it, and that was the kind of lighthearted mood everyone was in—before we reached Russia.

Our first stop after Vancouver had been Helsinki, 4,750 nautical miles away. I couldn't sleep during the nine-hour flight. The plane seating was cramped, and I was still emotionally keyed up.

The drive from the airport to the town of Helsinki reminded me of the raw beauty of Ontario—the countryside was rocky, with tall pines and the leaves beginning to turn on the deciduous trees. Our hotel room was comfortable, though we weren't used to the beds—no mattresses, just two or three inches of padding. In lieu of a radio, an intercom played old pop songs, vintage World War II, such as "I've Got a Gal in Kalamazoo." I decided that old songs never die, they just pipe them into hotels all over Europe.

Already the trip was turning out to be a mystery package, like a movie where the cast gets on a bus and no one—including the driver—knows the ultimate destination. Confusion abounded, all of it pleasant in a distracting way.

Team Canada encountered little competition in the games

against Finland and Sweden which were actually tune-ups for their heavy date with the Russians. But for the moment the pressure was off, and we could behave like tourists. We were invited to the home of the hotel manager, the only such visit we had on the entire trip, and we cherished it. The Mobergs had a lovely, old-world apartment, and the manager's wife, Pia, served wine and beer, chunks of cubed Swiss cheese, and salami. She showed us their sons' room, which was covered with hockey pennants and posters, most of them from the National Hockey League.

Before we took off for Russia, we put away enough food to feed a Chinese family of five for a year, took in the glorious countryside, had our first taste of caviar, and I, Colleen Howe, had a massage I will positively never forget.

We were invited on a tour of a cotton mill, but I passed, on the theory that their chances of making a comeback are slight. On the other hand, it seemed pointless to be in Finland and not take advantage of that ancient folk custom, the massage, which is native to that part of the world.

Everyone had been talking about the saunas and the massages, and I quickly decided that was just what I needed to restore the old physical tone. I called the hotel desk and was told to go right down. I walked into the clinic and said, "I'm Mrs. Howe. I have an appointment."

A burly, gray-haired woman in a white uniform nodded and motioned for me to sit down.

The next thing I knew a man came down a stairway, talked to her for a minute, and then gestured to me to follow. I thought, "What's this?" But I tagged along, a little uncertainly. He opened the door to a small room, pointed to a bare table, and told me to *undress*. Then he left.

I was getting very nervous. I mean, this was no time to play doctor. A troubling thought entered my mind: Why would *he* be telling me to get undressed, unless . . . no, couldn't be. The only other time I had ever paid for a massage was at a health club in Detroit where a masseuse, a woman, did a terrific job. But I was afraid that if I didn't hurry, get undressed and put something on, this whatever-he-was would walk in while I was in all my pristine glory.

Beginning to panic I looked around the room for a robe. There was a sheet on the table, but then I spotted some towels up on a high shelf. Naked, I climbed on a chair to get one. I reassured myself. "I'll put one of these on, then he'll take me to another room where I'm going to have a massage with all those other ladies in the waiting room and a nice, respectable, earth-mother type doing the rubbing."

But he walked back in, unannounced, and said brusquely, "Get on table."

I sputtered, "Are you the . . .the. . .uh. . .*masseur?*"

He grunted.

I lifted myself onto the table, afraid not to, afraid to leave, but thinking, "Migod, what am I going to do?"

I was beginning to wonder what kind of perverted place it was. But he went about his work quite matter-of-factly, and I forced myself—my body was as pliable as a steel rod—to relax, not wishing to appear to be your typical suspicious, nervous American. I was sure Europeans thought we were all so shy about our bodies. At the same time I was thinking, "Wait until Gordie hears about this."

As he kneaded my calves I thought, "Boy, if the girls could only see me now." He had the hands of a violinist. He started with my toes, my fingers, my arms, my legs. I began to wonder just how far the treatment went. The writer, Red Smith, once described a Finnish sauna and massage (administered by a lady) he had, at the end of which he said he was given a certificate attesting he was alive and clean.

"This," he said, "is partly true."

I skipped the sauna, but the massage was terrific *and*

respectable, and I couldn't wait to tell some of the other wives. I also had this mischievous desire *not* to give them the full story, other than to say how good they would feel and suggest that they try one. I had visions of how different ones would react. Marie Mahovlich, for one, is the epitome of a perfect, conservative lady. I believe she would have fainted dead away.

The extracurricular nonsense came to an end once we landed in Moscow. I used what Yankee ingenuity I had to make our hotel room at least livable. In the absence of disinfectant, I sprayed the floors and walls with underarm deodorant and cologne.

Unfortunately, no one had told me to pack Lysol. With a pair of pantyhose and a few packs of chewing gum as a bribe, I persuaded one of the scrubwomen to wash the bathroom floor. These strong, wrinkled peasant ladies are everywhere, and they work hard, though with little effect, since they do their scrubbing with huge buckets of dirty water. Nothing ever really gets clean.

We soon learned how popular hockey, and even American hockey players, were in Russia. Behind Lenin and the cosmonauts and the Bolshoi Ballet, they were maybe the next hottest thing. The scrub lady passed Gordie a note one morning with a Russian proverb on it which, translated roughly, meant good luck. Whenever we ventured down to the lobby there would be hundreds of autograph seekers. Wherever we went, the kids wanted to exchange pins with us.

Russians are very big on pins. They issue commemorative pins for almost any occasion — including the opening of a new school or supermarket. I was aware of this custom, so before we left the states I had a thousand "Howes of Houston" pins, campaign button size, made up with pictures of Gordie and the boys on them. Russian children would tag along beside us and say, "Gum! Gum!" or point to one of our pins and indicate they wanted to trade.

A photographer friend of ours, Mort Greenberg, who had arrived a few days earlier, told us we were terrible at playing the game.

"Look," he said, "if you have a small Team Canada button, you might exchange one for one. But those Howe buttons, they're unusual. You ought to get five for one." Gordie and I never had the heart to do it. The children weren't like the street beggars you encountered in Mexico. The whole pin negotiation was carried out on a very dignified level. If the kids started carrying on too much, the Russian soldiers broke it up. They were everywhere. They demanded—and got— complete respect and cooperation.

We arrived at Luzhniki Arena for game number five, the first of the series to be played in Moscow. After four games in Canada, the teams were even—not a good sign—at one win each and two ties. Outside the stadium it looked as if the Russians were gearing up for World War III. All the streets leading to the stadium were lined with soldiers standing two or three feet apart. I couldn't conceive of anything that could happen that would require the services of the entire Russian army.

Tickets for the stadium, which seated about 17,000, cost eight dollars and were sold out each night. As the stadium filled, the air was fragrant with the rich aroma of garlic, onions, and body odor. Deodorants have not really caught on with the Russian populace. As a type they are big and bulky and short on manners. Their diet is high in carbohydrates, and you seldom see a thin Russian.

We had to shove and push our way into the stadium. Once there, we found some surprises. The Luzhniki had a gigantic electronic scoreboard, much like the spectacular one at the Astrodome in Houston. At one end the board gave the results in English, at the other in Russian. Their scoreboard even gave the time in tenths of a second. The language barrier added a little color to the scene. When a pass set up the goal, the translation gave credit to the "assistant," rather than listing the standard "assist."

As I glanced around the stadium, I was struck again by the drabness of the scene, the lack of color. It was like looking at an old movie on television. All the spectators were dressed gray or brown or black—colorful consumer goods are hard to find in Russia. If our hotel rooms were poor, our seats at the game were dreadful. I couldn't imagine having traveled halfway around the world to sit in seats where you could see everything except either end of the ice.

From our seats, all we could observe clearly were the opening ceremonies, which were elaborate. Two young female figure skaters glided out and gave each team a loaf of bread, a traditional welcome. Then Russian children skated onto the ice and gave a single perfect rose to each player. It was one of the rare beautiful moments we enjoyed in Moscow.

The Russians scored first. Then Gordie connected with a slap shot that tied the game for Team Canada. When they announced his name they called him "Gordie Hooo." Mark was the "assistant." From then on, the cold war on ice raged. The Russians played a much more physical game at home than they had in Canada. During the third period Ralph Backstrom, who I think was the most consistent of the Canadian players, skated toward Kharlamov of Russia, who turned and kicked at Ralph's skates.

Kicking is one of the crudest tricks a hockey player can pull. It's the kind of maneuver little kids try until they learn there are absolute rules against it. We learned, soon enough, that the Russians were masters at it.

Backstrom took after the referee, Waldo Czapek of Poland, and I am sure with language that can best be described as *basic*, argued that the Russian, Kharlamov, be given a tripping penalty. Instead, Ralph received a ten-minute misconduct penalty. Amateurish refs plagued the series. Even with Mark scoring a goal, the Russians won that Moscow home opener, 3-2.

In a rather somber mood, we got up to leave the game. I noticed a trench coat draped over an empty seat beside me, and figuring it belonged to a Canadian in our group, I picked it up. As I was threading my way through the row of seats, a plainclothesman blocked my path. He began yelling in Russian and pointing to the coat. Frightened out of my wits, I tried to explain in broken sign language that I wasn't stealing the coat, I wasn't a spy, I loved vodka, and hadn't the faintest notion what he was shouting about.

Then a revolting thought hit me. What if the coat had been *planted* there? Just then some coins fell, either from the pocket of the coat or from my purse, which had dropped to the floor in my confusion. He yelled some more and pointed to the money. I didn't know if I was supposed to pick up the coins, offer them as a bribe, or what.

Finally, I pointed to the coat, told him *Nyet* with as much authority as I could, and tossed the coat into the nearest seat. He still didn't want to let me pass. I looked at him coldly—I believe I saw Lauren Bacall do that once to the Gestapo—and pushed past him. I never did find out what the Incident of the Trench Coat was all about.

It developed that nearly all of the people in the Team Canada were being confronted with small traumas. Dr. Wilson had bites all over his legs from the insects whose bed he seemed to have borrowed. The team dentist was stuck in the hotel elevator and later was heard to gasp, "If you think you've smelled body odors before, just get stuck in an elevator for forty-five minutes in this town."

In the middle of the night some men entered the room of Mr. Pattison, the owner of the Vancouver Blazers, and turned on the lights. They never said a word, but systematically began to search the room and the luggage, while he sat up in bed, stupefied. Another time, the wife of one of the officials emerged from a bath to find strange men searching through her belongings. Wearing a bath towel, she fled into the hall.

I decided the Russians were intentionally doing everything possible to irritate us, upset the players, and take their minds off the game. In short, they were trying to psyche us out, and they succeeded. Buses arranged to take us sightseeing would get lost or leave without us. One night there was an invitation to a cocktail party at the Canadian Embassy to be followed by an evening at the circus. We were exhausted, fed up with our treatment, and wanted no part of whatever new devilment the Russians had in store for us. We decided to boycott the planned entertainment. As it turned out, we missed the highlight of the whole trip. The Embassy served a complete buffet, the only decent food the team would have had, and the circus turned out to be a great deal of fun. Still, we hoped our boycott might improve matters.

Suddenly, the Russian chefs learned how to cook steaks, and an interpreter was assigned to sit with the wives at the games. Bill Hunter met with the Russian officials and told them flatly, "We have been harassed, and this must stop."

Not all the Russians were grim. There was one fellow whose real name was Alexander; we called him Odd Job, after a character in a James Bond movie. Odd Job was six-foot-four, weighed around 250, and was ideally suited to be a bodyguard. He looked as if could have gotten away with charging people just to let them live.

Odd Job was assigned to baby-sit with the Canadian players. Even though he had a head like a concrete block and a grim, almost morose expression, some of the players began to get friendly with him.

After lunch one day I started to walk out to the lobby, when Odd Job grabbed me by the arm and led me back into the dining room. My first thought was that I had not folded my napkin properly or had committed some other offense against the state. But Odd Job stopped at a table I hadn't noticed before, reached into a box, and handed me a large candy bar.

I said, "Why Alexander, thank you."

He smiled, jabbered a few words in Russian, then guided me back to the lobby.

Later, I told Gordie what a sweet gesture it was. "Don't kid yourself," he teased. "He's after your body, Colleen."

I told Gordie he had a dirty mind, and I loved him for it. But this was Odd Job's way of offering friendship. He was protective of the players and wanted to be liked by them. After one game, the Polish referee came aboard the bus and was giving the team a hard time—something I have never heard of a referee doing. Odd Job picked him up under the armpits and removed him like a piece of lint.

Tempers were short for game number six. The Russians scored within thirty seconds after the face off. It was evident our players were not in a very keen frame of mind, and the game ended, 5-2 in favor of the Russians. After the whistle blew, Rick Ley, a feisty veteran with the New England Whalers, squared off with Kharlamov. The Russians were outraged, demanding that Ley be put in *jail* for fourteen days, a common sentence for public disorders.

For once I had a decent seat and I learned something about the Russian character. They were crybabies. After the least little bump, they would lie on the ice like dead fish or go racing to the bench. I had never seen such dramatics. To inspire the team, and I suppose to impress the fans, they are not above a little raw stagecraft. Once their number ten limped off the ice with a knee injury. In full view of the crowd, the Russian trainer injected his knee right through the stocking. It was distasteful to watch but effective. The player braced himself as though someone were removing a bullet with a spoon, and the Russian fans went wild.

We left the arena that night a depressed and miserable lot.

Convinced that nothing was going to change, knowing the series—we were now down, three games to one with two ties—was beyond saving, we began to count the days until we could get out of Moscow. The next day, as a break in our routine, Gordie and I visited GUM, the Russian version of a modern department store. Gordie was mobbed by a group of people who closed in until they had backed him against the wall of a staircase.

Once we finally pried ourselves loose, we walked back to the hotel past the stands from which elderly, toothless but smiling ladies sold flowers for three rubles. We were in a hurry to get back to our room to rest because our photographer friend, Mort Greenberg, had somehow managed to get us tickets to see "The Nutcracker."

When we strolled into the lobby there was Mort, looking as though he were on the verge of tears. "This was the one thing I wanted to do for you," he said. "Now, after selling me the tickets, they tell me they are only good for tonight's performance if you are a teacher or a student in ballet."

Gordie and I tried to console Mort. Then he brightened and suggested that, instead, we see the circus we had missed earlier. In no time he had produced the tickets.

On the bus ride to the circus Gordie almost got into a fight. A man from Windsor, sitting in back of us, said idly, "I've gotten all the team's autographs except your son Marty. Haven't seen him around much."

"He's a little dejected," I said, honestly, "because he hasn't been playing, so he doesn't hang around the lobby much."

The man from Windsor nodded. "It's a shame Mark is so talented," he said. "Must make you feel badly that Marty hasn't got it and may never have."

There was a sound of breath being sucked in (mine), and I debated whether to tie into this thoughtless clod. But Gordie broke in first.

"Do you realize," he said, "what you have just said to the boy's mother? Don't you ever think before you open your mouth? Mister, if you say anything like that to my wife again, I'll flatten your nose." All the creeps weren't, after all, on *their* side.

When well-meaning people ask me how we keep Marty from feeling overshadowed, I never quite know what to answer. But Marty does.

"I'm glad for Mark," he says, "whatever he gets. I'm not trying to compete with him. I'd be crazy. Mark is a super player."

I think Marty is rather special. We no longer worry about his feeling slighted by Gordie's fame or the acclaim his brother has received. He has a maturity beyond his years.

The night of the circus we were assigned a Russian guide who made the rest of the trip a success. Had she been with us from the start, we might have departed with somewhat brighter feelings about the Soviet Union. There was a sad, poignant note to her life, and privately I ached for her. Her husband was a pilot whose comings and goings were determined by the state. She lived in a hostel because she lacked the permanent visa that would have entitled her to an apartment in Moscow.

Unable to obtain suitable lodging, she had to leave her son with her in-laws who lived hundreds of miles away. She had not seen her son in three years and her husband in four months. My heart went out to her. I knew the pangs of being separated from a child.

Even though her husband was due in Moscow the next day, she volunteered to appear at our hotel to explain Russian customs. She left in time to be on hand when he arrived. I was struck by her eagerness to please, and we developed a friendly and rewarding relationship.

Back at the arena, there was considerable pressure on

us—players and wives—on the day of the seventh game. The team knew it was back-to-the-wall time. The Russians had made Rick Ley apologize publicly for the fight that had occurred after the whistle. At the start of the game, they announced over the loudspeaker: "If there is any more dirty play on the part of Team Canada, the game will be canceled."

We expressed our disgust by cheering and applauding, a little hair of the dog that bit us. Instead of booing when they are unhappy, Russian fans whistle. We would have loved to pack up and go home that instant. But, of course, we couldn't. Ironically, Mark was cross-checked in the face in that game. How his jaw kept from being broken I'll never know.

The first chance he had, Gordie went after the Russian who nailed Mark and bounced him like a rubber ball. Later, Mark settled his own score. He whacked him one in the hand. Gordie noticed with some satisfaction, after the game, that the fellow was shaking hands with his left hand.

In the last seconds of the game, Bobby Hull flicked a pass into the goal, breaking a 4-4 tie and giving Team Canada a cliff-hanging win. We leaped from our seats, but our joy was short lived. The referee ruled that time had expired—the goal, he said, was scored after the clock had run out. I had been watching the timepiece. After the goal, the clock kept on running. The Russians called it a tie. In Canada, the newspapers reported it as a 5-4 win. It was an international joke.

With one game to go, the Russians had officially clinched the series. At a team meeting the next day, Bill Hunter angrily announced that, as far as Team Canada was concerned, we had won the game. There had been heated talk about calling off the final match and shipping out early. Hunter called for a show of hands of those who wanted to finish the series. To put Bill on a bit, the fellows had agreed not to raise their hands, although it was really unthinkable to quit. Only four or five raised their hands. Bill, who knew he was being had, smiled and said, "I see it's unanimous."

The Russians won the last game, 3-2, and the series by four games to one with three ties. At that point we were just relieved to have it done with and to be heading home. We did have a slight curiousity about what kind of celebration would be held in honor of the two teams. After the game, through word of mouth—there were no printed invitations—we heard there was to be a buffet at the hotel. Gordie was late getting back after signing autographs. As we headed for the buffet we passed some of the players moving in the other direction. They said not to bother.

No one was there to greet them. As was true of the entire series, they were not allowed to mix with the Russian players. As mementos or going away gifts, the Russians gave each Team Canadian a lacquered box with a picture of a faceoff on the top. Although attractive, they were packaged in boxes that smelled like limburger cheese. That night, the Russians' only interest was in getting some propaganda shots of Gordie and Bobby Hull with a few local big shots. They couldn't have cared less about paying tribute to the team.

Later that night, we slipped the "key ladies" a six-pack of beer and the team held its own party in the ninth floor hallway. There was still one meaningless stop on the way home, a game in Czechoslovakia, but the pressure was off, the party was over, and we knew it. There were no sad songs.

At the start of the trip we had received from merchants a supply of items not readily available to consumers in Russia, such as that most precious of goods, soft toilet paper. We decided to collect what we hadn't used and give it to Mort Greenberg's cousins. We filled plastic bags with all kinds of goodies. Mort was so touched he stood in front of us and cried. Mike Walton of the Minnesota Fighting Saints had found a tape recorder, and soft music was in the air.

"Oh, Mort, let's dance," I said, taking his hand. "I've been dying to dance all week."

We stayed up very late that evening. At that moment I think everyone connected with Team Canada felt very close, the way people do when they have endured some unusual experience together.

The next morning we left for Prague separately, the players on a Russian plane, the families on one provided by the Czechs. By this time I had been drawn very close to my friend, The Guide. Very simply, we had shared. As soon as I started to say good-by I felt myself choking up, the tears welling up in my eyes. I wished so much for her and wondered if our paths would ever cross again. She indicated it would not be wise for me to write her. I choked back more tears when she tapped on the bus window for one final farewell as the bus pulled slowly away from the curb in front of our hotel.

We were so happy and felt such a sense of release that we did not even complain about the separate plane bit. At 30,000 feet I kicked off my shoes. We had a lovely lunch, and for the first and only time I was served caviar. I settled into my seat and tried to collect my thoughts.

The trip had been a bitter disappointment, not just because Team Canada had lost the hockey series, but because of the general unpleasantness. We had expected too much, I suppose, but what should have been a glorious time turned into a test of nerves. I shudder to think what it will be like in 1980 at the Moscow Olympics unless the I.O.C. (the International Olympic Committee) insists on certain safeguards and concessions. The Russians are simply not prepared for the gaiety and freewheeling character of the massive Olympic crowds.

My thoughts drifted back to the few people I actually had met. The Guide, whose name I deliberately do not use. Odd Job. The old ladies at the flower stands. A young beautician, one of the few Russian women I encountered who tried to take pains in grooming herself. She was so grateful when I gave her a small, inexpensive pocket flashlight. I thought of all the faceless Russians I had seen walking the somber streets, the Russians no one had bothered to introduce. They could only offer to show us cold, barren buildings and tractor factories. There must be others, I thought, like The Guide and Odd Job, who wanted to share feelings and experiences but never had the chance.

After Czechoslovakia we were on the last lap home, a nine-hour-and-fifteen-minute flight to Toronto. We were aggrieved to find that the airline, unaware that hockey people are prodigious beer drinkers, had placed aboard only 65 cans to serve 200 thirsty souls. We all took sips out of a can, then passed it on to our neighbors. When the pilot announced that we were nearing Canadian soil all of us, as if on cue, started singing "Oh, Canada" and "Auld Lang Syne."

The Howes caught a connecting flight to Detroit to visit Murray and, with happy timing, to join the Aeros on an exhibition stop. We returned to find that one really dumb misunderstanding remained to be corrected. We did not know if our room had been wired for electronic eavesdropping or not. Whatever we might have suspected, we'd never had said so publicly.

When Gordie mentioned to reporters that there were bugs in our room, he meant insects, not listening devices.

So much for international intrigue.

10

How to Keep Everybody Happy (*Almost*)

THERE IS A CYCLE in sports in which the weak grow strong, and friends become enemies. It works in reverse, too, and often the lines get blurred.

I have seen it happen more than once in my time—my time dating back roughly to that of Joan of Arc.

So here we were again in Detroit, where the Aeros were to play the Michigan Stags, with my husband and sons returning as aliens to the city where we had lived so long and known so many moments of pure gladness. We were only a few days out of Russia, overjoyed to sleep once more in an authentic bed with a real mattress. I was on a tight schedule: planning to watch a minor game in which Murray was playing at 7:30 P.M., then catch the finish of the Aeros' contest against the Stags.

As I walked through the lobby of the hotel to pick up my car, I was aware of dozens of Secret Servicemen bustling around. They are so bland as to be conspicuous in their short hair, dark suits, and scrubbed faces. Then I remembered that the new President was in town for a dinner honoring Governor Milliken of Michigan. We had known both Gerald and Betty

Ford from years ago, when we used to take our kids skiing and bump into theirs on the slopes.

As the Secret Service types passed, I realized President Ford must be approaching. His limousine was parked out front. I had no expectation of getting near him, but as I heard the onlookers buzz I realized I was in his flight path.

As he reached the doorway he happened to glance over and said, "Well, hello, Colleen. Haven't seen you in a long time. How's Gordie?"

I told him we had just gotten back from the Soviet Union, and how marvelous it felt to be home. We had a new appreciation, I said, of all the advantages we had here.

He smiled and said, "I'm sure you do."

The president was wearing one of his WIN (Whip Inflation Now) buttons, and I teased him: "As sure as you've come out with a WIN button, someone will surely have to come out with a LOSE button."

"They probably already have," he said, laughing. With that he wished Gordie and the boys well and hurried off to the limousine behind his convoy of security men, who had been making impatient signs.

I stood there for a moment quite pleased with myself. A presidential welcome home! Now that was impressive. It was hard to believe that just two weeks had passed since we had made that apprehensive, sweaty-palmed landing at the Moscow airport.

Oh, did someone mention fear of flying? Let me tell you about mine, about how much I loved my husband, and how far it drove me, and what happens when fear and stubbornness and ice hockey collide.

I was absolutely petrified of airplanes during the early years of our marriage. But in 1956, I think it was, in the off season, Gordie agreed to a whirlwind six-week tour doing P.R. work for Eaton's department store in Canada. I was to join him in

Winnipeg, which meant flying. Days ahead of time I began to steel myself for the task. I practiced a kind of Hindu chant: I'm going to get on the plane, I'm going to get on the plane, I'm going to . . .

It was obvious to me even then that I had to overcome my terror of flying or resign myself to being a part-time wife and an untraveled one. I bought a set of lovely white luggage, decked myself out in new clothes, and kept trying to ignore my racing heart, which was going like a rivet gun.

I flew the first leg, from Windsor to Detroit, without a whimper. The flight was delightful, and I simply soared with new confidence. Inside me the urge just bubbled up to grab someone and say, "Look at me, I wasn't terrified, I just got off a flight and my legs aren't like wet noodles, and it was great, and I'm not afraid to fly anymore."

At Detroit we had to change to a plane for Toronto which would take us to Winnipeg and my waiting husband. We had been airborne only a few minutes when I glanced out the window and noticed how large the houses all seemed and how close the rooftops were. I wondered, idly, if the pilot planned to fly that low all the way to Winnipeg.

Then the pilot's voice came over the intercom, in that calm, low-keyed tone they always use when they are fumbling for their parachutes, and he said, "This is the captain speaking. We have encountered a slight mechanical problem, nothing to be concerned about, but we are going to jettison all our excess fuel to lighten the load and return to the Toronto airport. We'll be on the ground in a few minutes. Please fasten your seat belts."

Fasten your seat belts. Please remain seated until the plane has hit the side of the terminal building. Help. Get me out of this, God, and I'll never lose my temper again. I'll give up sweets. Anything.

I can't describe my fright, except to say that I couldn't get my mouth to work. The only thing that really saved me from hysteria was the panic of the woman sitting next to me. She was so outwardly afraid, and I was so inwardly afraid, we were the perfect pair. I spent so much time trying to compose her that it was my salvation. Before I could think about really embarrassing myself, we were back on the ground.

By then I had made up my mind that there was no way Colleen Howe would ever get back aboard that aircraft. I headed for the exit clutching all my paraphernalia—my hat, coat, handbag, and a large envelope containing letters I had intended to answer while cruising serenely through the clouds.

The stewards had been alerted that the wife of Gordie Howe was aboard, and as I started down the stairs one of them said, "Mrs. Howe, you needn't take all those things with you into the terminal. The repairs will only take a few moments, and the plane will be ready to reboard."

"Not with me on it, it won't," I assured him, and with head high I walked into the lobby, found the office of the airline, and asked if I could use a phone. "I'm terrified of flying," I said, "and I'm not getting back on that plane."

I was beginning to wonder now how I would ever get home. I felt a rush of relief when Gordie answered the phone. He already knew the flight had been delayed, that there had been a problem. The airline had called him.

"Colleen," he said, with a gentleness that always surprised and reassured me, "can you get back on that plane?"

I said no. I was to think of that forever after with an awful sense of my own immaturity. It was irrational. But I could not be expected to be sober and rational at the same time, given those circumstances.

"Look," Gordie said, "you stay put. I'll call Jack Gunn of the Eaton Company and his wife and ask them to come over and talk with you. Let that flight go on and perhaps you'll feel up to getting a later one."

The Gunns soon arrived and maneuvered me into the bar. I didn't hear a word they were saying because all I knew was that they wanted me to get on that plane and *it wasn't going to work.*

We had a drink, and another, and they waited for the alcohol to tranquilize me, but it didn't. So finally I said, "Look, I can't. I just can't. So don't feed me any more pep talk because it's hopeless."

After a long silence, Jack asked if I would agree to a train.

I thought quickly. Gordie would be leaving Winnipeg in the morning for Vancouver, and I'd have to catch up with him there.

"How long would it take by train?" I asked.

"Three days."

I stared into my cocktail glass. Three days. What would I do alone, on a train, for three solid days? The Gunns assured me I could load up on magazines, books, and crossword puzzles, and twenty minutes later we were pulling up to the railroad depot. They shoved me aboard, waved cheerfully, and disappeared slowly in the distance as the train moved out of the station. I thought, "Oh, Lord, what am I doing here on this train? For three days. I must be deranged."

At least, I wasn't afraid. Instead, I was only suffering from an advanced case of claustrophobia. The walls of my roomette were closing in on me. I threw open the door, found the conductor, and asked sharply, "Sir, can you tell me the first stop?" He said, "Parry Sound." I knew that was Bobby Orr's home town and thought it would be a suitable place from which to head back to Detroit.

I said, "Fine, I'll get off there."

The depot consisted largely of a small platform with four thin walls, a clerk in a green eyeshade sitting at a bare table, and two very worn benches. That was it. The hour was late, and it hadn't occurred to me, in my impetuosity, to ask if any other trains would pass through that night going back to Toronto.

The man in the green eyeshade, peering up at me curiously, said the next train to Toronto was at seven in the morning. My situation began to dawn on me, and it was not a cheery one. I couldn't call Gordie. He was in the air on his way to Vancouver, and there was no way to intercept him.

Just to brighten my mood, rain began to pound the roof, and lightning and thunder crackled and boomed. All I needed was to have some odd character appear in a horse-drawn carriage and tell me there was a castle on a hill with a room in it.

There I was, attractively tailored, with expensive luggage, a handsome husband waiting for me, but stranded on a platform in a town called Parry Sound, Ontario.

At that moment two very stern, tough-looking men walked into the depot and sat down. Suddenly, for the first time, it dawned on me how potentially dangerous my actions had been. I was tired and exhausted and on the verge of going to pieces. Almost twelve hours had gone by since I had left for the airport.

But there was *no way* I would allow myself to go to sleep in the same room with those two silent, ominous characters who were staring at me across the room. By this time, my imagination had turned them into some kind of assassins. I was wondering how they would dispose of my body. If one of them had so much as scratched an ear, I probably would have bolted for the door. I kept an eye on the clerk, praying that he wouldn't go off somewhere and leave me alone.

Morning finally came. My eyes were just about ready to bulge out of my head when the seven o'clock train to Toronto pulled in, and I staggered aboard. Back in Toronto, I made up my mind to rent a car and *drive* to wherever Gordie was by then. But first I called some friends, and on their advice checked into the Royal York Hotel across from the depot for a quick nap. I had been up for more than twenty-four hours and was ready to collapse.

I rented a room, threw myself into bed, and was asleep in seconds. I fell into one of those restless sleeps in which your dreams seem to incorporate all the strange sounds outside your door. The sounds persisted. *Something* woke me. I heard people screaming. I hurried to the window, raised it, looked out and stared, bewildered, at what I saw. Down on the street a crowd was gathering. In the rooms around me, people were knotting bedsheets and dangling them from the windows. The hotel was on fire.

At that moment, believe me, the light flashes before you. I thought, why didn't I get back on that plane? This whole thing was crazy. It was as though I had fallen into a time warp.

Dazed and a little shaken, I dashed to the phone, only to find that the switchboard had been abandoned. I could hear two girls in the next room having hysterics as they propped themselves on the window ledge. I moved to the open window and yelled at them not to be stupid; we could walk down. We were approximately six floors above the ground, and the firemen were lining up their nets below. The situation was getting more zany by the minute. But if I was afraid to get onto a plane, it was nothing compared to my feelings when I contemplated the prospect of diving out a window. I now knew the difference between fear and *real* fear.

We were talking to each other through the open windows—the girls next door and I. I told them to rip the sheets and blankets off the bed, get them dripping wet, then wrap themselves in the drenched blankets and stay by the window. I dashed to the door, thinking I might be able to see how thick the smoke was in the hallway. I opened the door a crack, and all I could see was a solid wall of black smoke. Immediately my lungs filled with the choking fumes, and I lurched back inside.

Shutting the door quickly, I began stuffing towels around the sides and bottom because I remembered my first aid training: In a fire most people die from asphyxiation.Then I tried to remember where I was on the floor in relation to the elevators. I regretted that I had been too punchy when I checked in to pay attention to such details.

Then it occurred to me that I was nearly at the end of a long hall and that there should be a stairwell. I put on my robe, wrapped a wet sheet around me, pulled open the door and crawled out of the room on my hands and knees. Smoke swirled above me, and I heard the distant sounds of screaming. I scrambled along the corridor rug until I found an exit door. I turned the knob and it opened. To my amazement, I saw that I was at the top of a long flight of stairs, and there was no smoke. It was like a fire stairway. I ran down the steps, from floor to floor, and ended up in a huge kitchen and from that point found my way into the lobby.

Well, it was a madhouse, with guests in their pajamas and wet bedsheets and scared out of their wits. Firemen with long, wriggling hoses hurried through to various stairways and moved out of sight, and from upper floors came loud shouts and the crunch of fire axes. As it turned out, the hotel didn't suffer any extensive damage, and no guests were seriously injured. The big danger was that people would panic in their frenzied efforts to get out of their rooms.

I wandered around for a while, as confused as the others, wanting to talk to someone but afraid of mentioning my name and having Gordie read that I was in a fire in Toronto.

In an hour the blaze, which had started on one of the floors below mine, was extinguished, and the smoke slowly dissipated. Crazy as it sounds, I returned to my room and went back to sleep. The next day everything I owned smelled as though it had been steam pressed in a barbecue pit.

After all the excitement, confusion, and frustration I had experienced, I finally gave up and went back to Detroit and waited for Gordie to come home. I'm not sure there is a point to all this, or that it served any useful purpose, but it did cure my fear of flying. I had gone through planes, trains, and a fire trying to reach my hockey player, and if that isn't what marriage is all about, what is?

I do not admit defeat easily, and to the degree that the kids have this quality I hope they get it from me as well as Gordie. If there is any other emotion besides love that makes the Howes tick it would be pride. It was pride that kept Gordie on top for as long as he played hockey. We have tried to instill it in our children—not the pride that makes you do unnecessary things, but the kind that drives you to compete.

Perhaps we sound like the last of the Goodie Two Shoes. If we are, I accept the label without apology. Not that our marriage, mine and Gordie's, hasn't had a crisis or two or that we haven't had our share of family donnybrooks. But as old-fashioned as it sounds, we actually like each other. We enjoy working together and being together. It is a high compliment, I think, to have two young men making the kind of money Marty and Mark do, choosing to live at home.

When Gordie and I are invited to give speeches we usually base them on what we call our LSD philosophy. That often produces a mild shock in the audience until we explain that we are talking about Love, Sacrifice, and Dedication. It's important to love what you are doing. If you have that the rest isn't so difficult—the part about sacrificing and dedicating yourself to a course or a goal.

Surely, every parent hopes his or her child will grow up, if not to be president of the United States, at least to be a good and useful citizen. And I think all parents hope and worry, if their kids will like them as much at age twenty as they did when they were toddlers begging for hugs and squeezes.

One particular night—just a very ordinary moment, really—made me understand that the Howe family had something special going for it.

During the fall of 1974, Gordie and the boys went off on what seemed to be a record road trip lasting sixteen or seventeen days. It was as though they had gone to the Crusades. Cathy and I were more excited than usual to have them back at last, and to have a male presence in the home.

Mark, in fact, said, "Gee, I've been gone so long I can't remember what's in my closet."

After all the hugs and kisses and glad-to-be-homes, I expected to see the boys take off for brighter lights, a few beers, an evening with friends, or whatever. After all, they had been flying in the same planes, staying at the same hotels, practicing the same plays, and playing in the same games as their father. They were entitled to a little liberty.

Instead, they challenged Mom and Dad to a game of bridge. While Cathy worked on her geometry problems and our pet, Skippy, snoozed on the floor, Mark and Marty and Gordie and Colleen played cards. I realized that night that togetherness was more than a word.

We don't have any special formula for happiness. I don't think we are that much different from thousands of other families, except that the men in ours work at jobs that are performed in front of people who can grade them.

I suppose the six articles of Satchel Paige, the legendary old barnstorming pitcher, have become the most quoted set of rules since the Ten Commandments. The most famous of all was the one that went, "Don't look back, something might be gaining on you."

Any tips or household hints I might offer will not be that profound. But they worked for us.

The doctor who delivered all four of our children, Dr. James Matthews, often was my confidante and adviser. He once gave me a guideline I have tried to remember and practice whenever I find myself struggling to cope.

Jim said, "Colleen, just think of your life as a scale. And when you see the scale getting unbalanced, you can tell yourself something is wrong. You can tell if you are not spending enough time with your husband, or your children, or enough just on yourself. If you can keep *your* scale balanced, so will your family."

Too often mothers and wives, I think, tend to shortchange themselves. They spread themselves so thin that they neglect their own needs. Then they become martyrs, or feel like martyrs, and everyone is unhappy.

Rule 1. A wife and mother has to retain her self-esteem.

Marriage for many people can become a locked-in situation. For me it has not. Gordie has allowed me whatever freedom I needed, and more. He has treated me as an individual, not as someone, or thing, he can dictate to or own. I am not the fifth *child* in our family. Gordie and I learned something many couples forget, that we needed to save time just "for us." It became more difficult as Gordie's name and fame and responsibilities grew.

Rule 2. The respect parents show each other will be passed on to their children.

One night, before a Red Wing game, Gordie promised me, "I don't care who makes what plans after the game. We're not joining anybody anywhere. *We're* going out." We went to a restaurant with a piano bar, and I was feeling very romantic. In fact, downright sexy. Then along came a drunken fan who plopped himself down at our table. Gordie and I looked at each other. We both knew there was no way this fellow was going to leave, short of Gordie slugging him. So we shrugged, relaxed, and actually enjoyed the company of the fan, who turned out to be a rather hilarious character. And he never once left the table during the entire evening.

We laughed about our evening "alone" on the way home. But, fortunately, there were many other sweet, fanless nights.

Time has always been so short for us, we sometimes had difficulty deciding whether we needed to spend it in each other's company or with the children. We would be torn between wanting the kids and needing time to ourselves.

The after-the-season vacation was a typical choice. Gordie and I tried a couple of times to head for Florida alone, so he could unwind and I could get to know my husband, who had been on the road so much—always for most of the last month if the Red Wings had been in the Stanley Cup play offs.

After a day or two, Gordie would start missing the kids. Then I would. Suddenly, we'd find ourselves homesick in balmy Florida, and we'd end up flying home after just one week of a vacation that was scheduled to last two.

Rule 3. When you crave privacy, either bury your guilt or plan around it.

We finally found a remedy. We would take the kids with us for a week, so they could spend time with their Dad. Then we'd pack them aboard a plane and ship them home. The second week could be enjoyed with pure hearts, no homesickness, and blessed privacy. And the kids knew we needed and wanted some time alone.

With four children in the family, I also found it important that each have his or her time alone with Gordie and me. It was also important that all four have time with their Dad and without me. I deliberately stayed home from some fishing trips for that very reason.

Gordie's own father had to work such long, hard hours to

survive that Gordie didn't get to know him until he was full-grown, a fact that both always regretted. Our kids also had to learn that at certain times one of them was going to get more of my attention than the rest. When Mark was preparing to leave for the Olympics, the others knew and understood that I had to put my full efforts behind his trip.

Rule 4. In raising children, the crucial thing isn't to treat them equally but to treat them fairly.

Gordie and I are disciplinarians by instinct, but I don't believe we have been too harsh. Children, as well as adults, need to be told when they are wrong or off base. At the same time, I also felt our children had certain rights, such as privacy. And I tried never to invade that privacy. I wanted them to know Gordie and I were there to listen when they needed to talk, but not to interfere.

Rule 5. Don't be afraid to give your kids time and room in which to retreat. You can expose them, like flowers, to too much sunlight.

We never held anything our children cherished over their heads as punishment. Because of this policy I think they respected us even when they were being admonished. We never said, "If you don't make good grades, you aren't going to get to play hockey." On their sixteenth birthdays we have given each the use of a car, but we have never used the car as a weapon. I have always disliked the idea of giving children something, then using it as a threat the minute they misbehave.

Rule 6. Don't use as pawns—for favor or punishment—the objects or courtesies your children enjoy most.

If we have had any self-enforcing rule in our home, it was this: You were better off if you told on yourself. If you came to us and admitted what you had done, the punishment would invariably be lighter because of the courage behind the confession. But if we heard it from some other source, or if you lied . . .

I will never forget the sight of Cathy running from the creek toward the house one day as though her life depended on it. Mark was in hot pursuit behind her. She and a friend had tried smoking and her brother Mark had caught them. He said, "I'm going to tell Mom."

Cathy made a beeline for the house, as fast as her young legs would carry her. She darted in the door and burst out, "Mom, I was smoking. Mark saw me. But I'll never do it again." It turned out that Mark had been teasing, hadn't intended to squeal at all. But Cathy knew she had best get to me first, just in case.

Rule 7. Conscience is the best policeman.

I don't know if we could be called demanding parents or not. But I do think it is as great a sin not to expect enough from your children as to expect too much. Gordie believes in being Number one. So do I. Our efforts start with that. It is true that goals can be set so impossibly high as to discourage honest effort. But kids need to know that failing isn't a tragedy. Not trying is.

Rule 8. Encourage your kids to test themselves, to compete, to find their limits. Let them learn that effort counts as well as performance.

All along, we have maintained that whatever the Howes did, it should be fun. That was one reason Gordie played as long as he did; it is the same reason he quit when he did in Detroit in 1971. Once, when we sat down with the boys to discuss their investments, I pointed out that they wouldn't have hockey to depend on forever.

Mark looked at me thoughtfully. "I wouldn't mind that," he said, "playing hockey forever. I like what I'm doing. I love it."

Rule 9. You don't have to excel at something, but you should enjoy it enough to give 100 percent, whether it is for money or exercise or to feed the spirit.

Over the years, a controversy has raged over a type of parent known as the stage mother and in more recent years, the Little League mother. It carries over into hockey, but I have found these people—identified as pushy, obnoxious, wild-eyed with fervor—to be the exception, not the rule. No, you don't want to drive your sons or daughters into the ground. But you do have an obligation to provide as much guidance and exposure and assistance as your time and talents will allow. I think you should try to stimulate them. For us it was hockey. It gave us an interest to share, and it helped our children grow physically and mentally.

Our kids weren't angels. We got the usual call from the school principal or from the man at the hardware store, where Mark and a pal had snitched some Magic Markers. We quarrel. We blow off steam. We behave selfishly. But when it happens, we have the knack of clearing the air fast, and we do not let hurts or grudges linger.

My family has made me the proudest wife and mother in captivity. The successes of Gordie and Mark and Marty are well chronicled. But as far as I am concerned there are *four* hockey players in the Howe family. Murray, so much younger, has been in the background, and being separated from the rest of us wasn't easy. But, at fourteen, he was a little trouper who worked hard for what he hopes will lead to his own pro career.

Being the only girl among the Howe kids wasn't an easy assignment, but Cathy has shown talent in art, music, track, and swimming, in an era when girl athletes and career women command new respect. She rides a Honda so well we call her the Debbie Lawler of the Howe gang.

Cathy and Murray were the ones, inevitably, who had their names left out of articles or misspelled. But both survived without damages to their egos. From the time they were infants, I had hoped that all our children would grow up to be good citizens, that they would love and care about people and have respect for themselves. They have not disappointed me.

Rule 10. You can invent a game, but not love. Give it generously to those around you.

I have often paused to wonder how much good can happen to one family. I've been blessed with healthy children and a talented husband and experiences beyond wishing. In the spring of 1973, Gordie and I were among the guests attending a state dinner at the White House, honoring Haile Selassie, then the Emperor of Ethiopia. I came unglued when I opened the invitation, embossed with the presidential seal, and we accepted eagerly.

Many memories of that night still flash into my mind at the slightest tug: standing together in front of the mirror, giving ourselves a last-minute inspection, thinking what a handsome couple we were, how grand Gordie looked in a black tie; bumping into Don Newcombe, the ex-baseball great, and relaxing to find at least one other athlete among the eighty-odd guests: Gordie getting eyestrain from Zsa Zsa Gabor's cleavage; and being introduced in the formal receiving line, to the president of the United States, as Mr. and Mrs. Gordon Howe, of Bloomfield, Michigan.

And Richard Nixon replying, "Oh, no, this is Gordie Howe of the Detroit Red Wings."

We watched him later, from a distance, curiously, this embattled president who in less than a year would resign from office. Watergate was even then a storm unchecked. But he seemed relaxed and unharried. We stayed until the late hours, long after the Nixons and the emperor had retired, dancing and drinking champagne. The sport of ice hockey had indeed carried Gordie Howe and his family farther than time and space.

We have lived a lifetime sharing the fun and closeness and rewards not available to many families. I know Gordie wishes he had, say, five more years to give to hockey. Five, because he could then wait around for Murray, my fourth hockey player. But we both know that won't happen. There is, after all, a limit to how long and how hard one can cheat the calendar.

One night in Houston at the end of the 1974 season when we were all enjoying a dinner out, we got a glimpse of the future. There had been a rock show or something, and all the teenagers were jamming into the restaurant.

A group of them spotted Mark, and after a few moments one left his friends and walked over to our booth. "Don't you play hockey," he said to Mark, "for the Houston Aeros?"

No one in the group had even looked at Gordie. Mark turned to his father and smiled. "Dad," he said, "it's time to retire."

Gordie laughed. We all did. But I knew exactly what he was thinking. *No regrets.* Whenever the time came. He had been asked, I don't know, a thousand times what it was like to play on a side with his two older sons, and he can't give you a great galactic flash because Gordie Howe isn't that kind of man.

So what he says, softly with his eyes shining, for all of us, is this:

"Maybe three days, three years, or ten years from now, it is something I can talk about the rest of my life. It was a pretty nice thing to go on the road to do your job and be able to take half of your family with you."

Howe Professional Records

Gordie Howe

Season	Club	League	Regular Schedule GP	G	A	P	PM	Playoffs GP	G	A	P	PM
1945–1946	Omaha	USHL	51	22	26	48	53	6	2	1	3	15
1946–1947	Detroit	NHL	58	7	15	22	52	5	0	0	0	18
1947–1948	Detroit	NHL	60	16	28	44	63	10	1	1	2	11
1948–1949	Detroit	NHL	40	12	25	37	57	11	*8	3	*11	19
1949–1950	Detroit	NHL	70	35	33	68	69	1	0	0	0	7
1950–1951	Detroit	NHL	70	*43	*43	*86	74	6	4	3	7	4
1951–1952	Detroit	NHL	70	*47	39	*86	78	8	2	*5	*7	2
1952–1953	Detroit	NHL	70	*49	*46	*95	57	6	2	5	7	2
1953–1954	Detroit	NHL	70	33	*48	*81	109	12	4	5	9	*31
1954–1955	Detroit	NHL	64	29	33	62	68	11	*9	11	*20	24
1955–1956	Detroit	NHL	70	38	41	79	100	10	3	9	12	8
1956–1957	Detroit	NHL	70	*44	45	*89	72	5	2	5	7	6
1957–1958	Detroit	NHL	64	33	44	77	40	4	1	1	2	0
1958–1959	Detroit	NHL	70	32	46	78	57	—	—	—	—	—
1959–1960	Detroit	NHL	70	28	45	73	46	6	1	5	6	4
1960–1961	Detroit	NHL	64	23	49	72	30	11	4	11	*15	10
1961–1962	Detroit	NHL	70	33	44	77	54	—	—	—	—	—
1962–1963	Detroit	NHL	70	*38	48	*86	100	11	7	9	*16	22
1963–1964	Detroit	NHL	69	26	47	73	70	14	*9	10	*19	16
1964–1965	Detroit	NHL	70	29	47	76	104	7	4	2	6	20
1965–1966	Detroit	NHL	70	29	46	75	83	12	4	6	10	12
1966–1967	Detroit	NHL	69	25	40	65	53	—	—	—	—	—
1967–1968	Detroit	NHL	74	39	43	82	53	—	—	—	—	—
1968–1969	Detroit	NHL	76	44	59	103	58	—	—	—	—	—
1969–1970	Detroit	NHL	76	31	40	71	58	4	2	0	2	2
1970–1971	Detroit	NHL	63	23	29	52	38	—	—	—	—	—
1973–1974	Houston	WHA	70	31	69	100	46	13	3	14	17	34
1974–1975	Houston	WHA	75	34	65	99	84	13	8	12	20	20
Detroit and NHL Totals			*1687	*786	*1023	*1809	1643	154	67	91	158	218

*—League-leading figure

Hart Memorial Trophy (MVP), 1951–1952, 1952–1953, 1956–1957, 1957–1958, 1959–1960, 1962–1963.

Art Ross Trophy (Top Scorer), 1950–1951, 1951–1952, 1952–1953, 1953–1954, 1956–1957, 1962–1963.

Lester Patrick Trophy (Outstanding Service to U.S. Hockey), 1967.

Gary L. Davidson Trophy (MVP), 1973–1974.

1st All-Star Team 1950–1951, 1951–1952, 1952–1953, 1953–1954, 1956–1957, 1957–1958, 1959–1960, 1962–1963, 1965–1966, 1967–1968, 1968–1969, 1969–1970, 1973–1974, 1974–1975, 1975–1976.

2nd All-Star Team, 1948–1949, 1949–1950, 1955–1956, 1958–1959, 1960–1961, 1961–1962, 1963–1964, 1964–1965, 1966–1967.

Record for . . .

most Hart Memorial Trophies (6); most Art Ross Trophies (6); most career seasons (25); most career games (1,687); most career goals (786); most career assists (1,023); most career points (1,809); most career winning goals (122); most career games including playoffs (1,841); most career goals including playoffs (853); most career assists including playoffs (1,114) most career points including playoffs (1,967); most years in playoffs (19), (co-holder); most points in a playoff final series (12), 1954–1955; most goals in a playoff semi-final series (8), 1948–1949; fastest goal from start of a playoff game (nine seconds), 1953–1954 (co-holder); most All-Star team selections (24); most consecutive All-Star team selections (15); most 1st All-Star team selections (15); most All-Star Games played (22); most All-Star Game goals (10); most All-Star Game assists (8); most All-Star Game points (18); most All-Star Game penalty minutes (25); most All-Star Game penalties (11); most points in one All-Star Game (4), 1965 (co-holder).

Mark Howe

			Regular Schedule					Playoffs				
Season	Club	League	GP	G	A	P	PM	GP	G	A	P	PM
1970–1971	Detroit Jr. Wings	SOJHL	44	37	*70	*107	—	—	—	—	—	—
1971–1972	Detroit Jr. Wings	SOJHL	9	5	9	14	—	—	—	—	—	—
1971–1972	U.S.A. Olympic Team											
1972–1973	Toronto Marlboros	Jr. "A" OHA	60	38	66	104	27	—	—	—	—	—
1973–1974	Houston Aeros	WHA	76	38	41	79	20	14	9	10	19	4
1974–1975	Houston Aeros	WHA	74	36	40	76	30	13	10	12	22	—
Major League Totals			**150**	**74**	**81**	**155**	**50**	**27**	**19**	**22**	**41**	**4**

Lou Kaplan Award (Rookie of the Year), 1973–1974
2nd All-Star Team, 1973–1974

Marty Howe

			Regular Schedule					Playoffs				
Season	Club	League	GP	G	A	P	PM	GP	G	A	P	PM
1970–1971	Detroit Jr. Wings	SOJHL										
1971–1972	Toronto Marlboros	Jr. "A" OHA	56	7	21	28	122	—	—	—	—	—
1972–1973	Toronto Marlboros	Jr. "A" OHA	38	11	17	28	81	—	—	—	—	—
1973–1974	Houston Aeros	WHA	73	4	20	24	90	14	1	5	6	31
1974–1975	Houston Aeros	WHA	75	13	21	34	89	11	—	2	2	11
Major League Totals			**148**	**17**	**41**	**58**	**179**	**25**	**1**	**7**	**8**	**42**